Reviews of *The Ki*

"FRESH, INSPIRING, TRUE - and most of all, practical! So many Christian books give lots of great thoughts and theories for you to ponder and mull over, but that is generally where they stop. Paul expertly puts practical application of well thought out ideas into your head that you can take out and use immediately. Get ready to enter the Kingdom mindset, challenge yourself, and get tons of encouragement as you read Paul's writing." Walker Clan - 5 Stars

"REAL FAITH...REAL TEACHING - This book series is continually encouraging the every day Christian to take a step back at what is called the norm in Christian living and understand the heart behind it all. Have you ever wondered where the 'line' is in certain areas of life... like watching movies or music, helping your kids understand what is right and wrong? Paul Gibbs places Kingdom Principles to live by... not rules and regulations...liberty not slavery. Highly recommended for the Christian seeking to go further...two thumbs up!" Tim Ro - 4 Stars

"DEEP AND IMPACTFUL! - This book can help you to find the seeds that have been planted, watered, and that God is wanting to grow in you! Your purpose in life will become more clear! Through this book, I have gained so much insight into how to live the abundant life that God desires for all of us to have! To leave this world a better place than when I entered it." Stephanie - 5 Stars

"THIS IS A MUST READ - A fantastic book which really makes you think and explore ideas to a deeper level. Such a quick and easy read due to the layout and content. The personal stories told are really engaging, whilst helpful in explaining the desired point. Read this book if you want to be challenged, inspired, and encouraged - you won't regret it!" Holly - 4 Stars

"INSPIRING AND CHALLENGING BOOK - It is an easy read with simple style of writing but with deep questions and thoughts. Many times I had to just pause to process the thought or allow my mind to process the question and to unpack it...A great book that anybody choosing to live for God should read." Dan Ran - 5 Stars

"A MUST READ! - This book challenged me to dig deeper into the Father's heart as it distinguished between religion and faith. Ultimately I would recommend this book to anyone who desires to see day-to-day questions we ask through God's eyes rather than our own, strives to be an instrument in the furthering of the Kingdom of God, and yearns to be captivated by a renewed love for the Father. Overall, it was an amazing book and I would encourage you to take the time to read it!" Elle Marie - 5 Stars

"ABOVE THE LINE - If you are interested in learning about the heart of God, you need to read this book. I know a lot of people who have dismissed God because they believe He is a cosmic-killjoy, but this book will help them see the true heart of the God of the Bible and give them an appetite to dig into the Bible and gain more insight as to who God really is. It is easy to read and very thought provoking. Excellent book!!" Misha - 5 Stars

"USEFUL AND PRACTICAL - In the process of beginning anything new, fresh, or different, I think everyone goes through stages of the process. The problem is, no one knows what the stages are, until now. Paul does an excellent job of breaking down the stages of pioneering, using simple terms and analogies that are practical in nature and Biblical in scope. The best part about the book is that it is not just information, but it actually helps the pioneer in whatever stage he/she is in." Carl - 5 Stars

"BE FOREWARNED - Gibbs' challenging thoughts on vision and leadership make me uncomfortable. It is not always easy to see where I am within the four stages of pioneering, or even to see my personal vision for my efforts in the Kingdom in High Definition . . . but this story and challenge offer me a lens. It has given perspective to the early years of my journey, and in some places has unpacked the vague feelings and thoughts that were floating around in my head and my heart almost anonymously." Chris - 5 Stars

"READ IT!! - This book inspired me, moved me, and challenged me on things I had not even thought about before!" Judith - 4 Stars

"CATCHING THE PIONEERING SPIRIT - What's great about this book is that it's real stories about real people; it is their successes and failures. It is an inspirational book about a grassroots organization that has risen to have a Global influence but also gives the reader clear, practical advice. Although written from a Church ministry perspective, I can imagine that pioneers from different walks of life could find themselves in one of the four stages of a pioneer and also find hope and direction that will help enable them to take their dream into a reality." Pete - 5 Stars

"I HAVE BEEN SO BLESSED BY THE BOOK - After feeling very led to purchase it, I gave [my first copy] away after reading the first few incredible pages. Thoughts of myself said, I'm not a pioneer. I am a helper, a person who helps other people with their vision.... And then, I let God tell me what He thought of me. He brought to remembrance things placed in my heart long ago." Tifany - 5 Stars

*Reviews for The Kingdom Trilogy book series by Paul Clayton Gibbs. Used by permission from Amazon. Look for *Kingdom Principles: Develop Godly Character* and *Kingdom Pioneering: Fulfill God's Calling* on amazon.com.

PAUL CLAYTON GIBBS

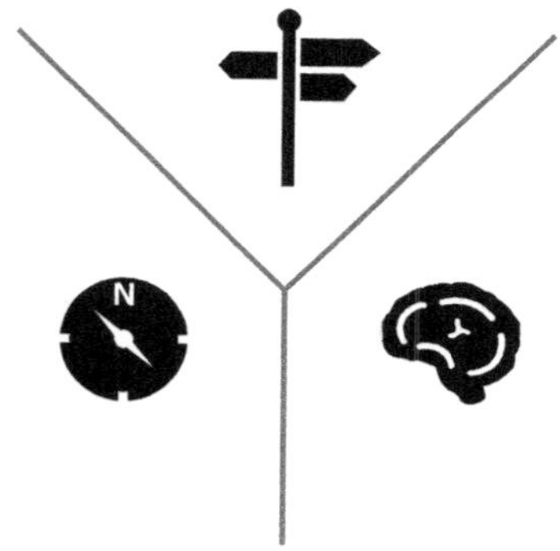

KINGDOM PATTERNS

find God's direction

KINGDOM PATTERNS: Discover God's Direction
(A previous version of this book was titled THE SEED AND THE CLOUD: The Kingdom Patterns)

Published by Harris House Publishing
www.harrishousepublishing.com
Colleyville, Texas
USA

Available on amazon.com and paismovement.com/resources.

This title is also available in other formats.
Cover creation and design by Paul Green and Paul Clayton Gibbs/ revised by Andrew Sherrington.
Author's photo by Dino Gilley © 2014.

Library of Congress Cataloging-in-Publication Data

Gibbs, Paul Clayton, 1964 -
KINGDOM PATTERNS: Discover God's Direction / Paul Clayton Gibbs
p.cm.
Includes bibliographical references
ISBN 978-1-946369-28-4 (pbk.)
1. Christianity and Culture. 2. Christian Life. I. Title.
BR115.C8G53 2016
261 - dc22

Printed in the United States of America.

For Lynn
my best friend
"number 9"

To my wonderful Pastoral Board who have helped my family and me on my journey through all of these Patterns. You have encouraged us, supported us, laughed with us, and helped me to share the vision of the Kingdom with so many.

Wayne, Terry, Dan, Kelly, Jim, Kim, and Stephen

My thanks to

The Foxy Lynn for being with me every step of the way

Joel and Levi for being the greatest sons on the planet

Andrew Sherrington for your work revising the book cover

David Tiede for taking my illustrations and giving them a more professional feel

The Pais:Global Team for resourcing the world as they seek God first

The Pais National Directors for empowering the pilgrimage of our apprentices

Harris House Publishing for seeking God's Kingdom first and your business second

KINGDOM PATTERNS

The Question for a Pilgrim

Seed

There is a line.[1]

Many of us live on this line between the extremes of fear and fortune. It represents the laws, rules, and regulations of Christianity. As line-dwellers, we look at one end of the line and ask how far we can go without getting into trouble, and at the other end, how far we must go in order to be rewarded. This line is horizontal, not vertical, and it can never take us upwards because laws help us know where we are failing but they lack the power to help us succeed.

Then there is a cloud.

In God's Word, clouds are connected to His dream for His people. The cloud that directed Israel to the Promised Land, the cloud that will be at Jesus' return[2], the cloud that symbolizes our eventual dwelling with Him.[3] God's desire is that we break through a life dominated by His laws by reaching for a life lived for His dream. Yet the journey to live above the line starts below it.

There is a seed.

It is the eternal purpose God buried in you before you even knew Him.

> *He has also set eternity in the human heart . . .* [4]

When a pilgrim first receives a vision, it is not the finished concept and is therefore not fully understood. It is just a seed. A seed is not the plant. It does not taste like the plant, look like the plant, or feel like the plant. Yet it contains within it everything required to *become* the plant.

God puts that seed of purpose in our hearts, and His dream gives it something to reach for, something for our souls to be drawn to and something for our souls to connect to. Yet one more thing is required for our God-given purpose to adhere with God's vision: a training stake.

And so there exists Kingdom Patterns.

The Kingdom Patterns provide a support to help the purpose God placed within you grow safe and strong. They are not intended to restrict you but are designed to guide your growth. They are not artificial nor static . . . They are organic.

Each of the five patterns I have chosen for this book will be taught in three stages:

> *The Pattern:* I will show a diagram to depict the journey you may go through.
>
> *The Pilgrim:* I will use a Bible character to reveal the purpose for the pattern.
>
> *The Practices:* I will provide advice to apply along the way.

KINGDOM PIONEERING: Fulfill God's Callng, KINGDOM PRINCIPLES: Develop Godly Character, and now *KINGDOM PATTERNS: Discover God's Direction*. All three books of *The Kingdom Trilogy* can be read in any order, and every one of them requires a passion to live for God's Kingdom. They are for you who are seeking to bond your hearts with God's and bind your dreams to His. In doing so, you will discover that many of your own desires were planted there by Him in the first place.

Bubble

Have you ever lost Jesus?

Some of the best people have.

> *Every year Jesus' parents went to Jerusalem for the Festival of the Passover.*[5] *When he was twelve years old, they went up to the festival, according to the custom. After the festival was over, while his parents were returning home, the boy Jesus stayed behind in Jerusalem, but they were unaware of it.*[6]

At first they had no clue that Jesus was missing, but once they did . . .

> *. . . they began looking for him among their relatives and friends.*[7]

Have you ever felt that God was not where you expected Him to be? Have you ever lost a sense of connection and therefore a sense of purpose? Have you ever lost track of His direction in your life? Sometimes when we feel this has happened, we make the same mistake as Jesus' parents. We look for Him in the wrong place. We search among our friends and relatives.

It's human nature. So, when I ask someone to consider an opportunity, I *bubble* them.

You see, I find that when some people are presented with a decision or opportunity, they might say, "I will pray about that." But they don't. At least, not at first. Instead, they search for God's direction among those they love or respect. After they've done that, then they get around to prayer and reflection, but by that time their hearts and minds are no longer virgin territory. Their souls have been impregnated by everyone else's opinions, and the task of recognizing the Holy Spirit becomes more difficult.

So I put them in a bubble. I make them promise not to talk to a single soul until they have first asked themselves a particular question, which I will share with you later. Then after an agreed upon period of time, I encourage them to inquire of others. The emphasis of my 'bubble wrap' is to help people go on a journey with God, rather than take a shortcut with their nearest spiritual guru or make a pit stop with a friend.

After all, we, like Joseph and Mary, are pilgrims.

> *A pilgrim is one who travels to a sacred place for religious reasons.*[8]

Yet so many of us seem lost. I cannot tell you how many great and godly leaders I have sat down with in a coffee shop and listened to their lost-ness, their questions of: What's happening? What am I doing? Why am I here? What's next? What's the plan?

And this crisis of *fate* is a problem.

Why? Because we are made in the image of God. And why are we made in the *image* of God? So we can help others *imagine* God.

I find that inspiring.

But I also find it awkward.

I am concerned that a fragmented, disjointed life may offer up an image of a flaky, dysfunctional God. One who is unsure what to do with us. One who toys with us in a lifelong game of spiritual hide and seek. That is not the image of God I want my life to project, and although I may not have all the answers to my colleagues' questions, I do have an inkling of a pilgrim's process. It is a process that starts with a better question than the ones we usually ask.

In order to share this question with you, however, let me ask you another. If we are to live by faith and not by fate, then *where* is this sacred 'place' that we are supposed to be heading?

Map

Perhaps there is a clue in the journey of the first pilgrim in God's story.

> *The Lord had said to Abram, "Go from your country, your people and your father's household to the land I will show you. I will make you into a great nation, and I will bless you; I will make your name great, and you will be a blessing."*[9]

Abram's expedition was the first religious pilgrimage.

Among the places he went was Salem, the future site of Jerusalem. Abram's journey reminds me of a medieval map that was created for Christians traveling to the Holy Land in the Middle Ages. It shows four circles, one at the center and the other three fanned out around it. The center circle represents Jerusalem, and the other three display Europe, Africa, and Asia.[10]

It exhibits the mistake we make on our own pilgrimage.

Symbolically, it depicts the idea that the search for God is a place, a target, a geographical bullseye that we must endeavor to reach. Maybe this concept is what causes us to ask the weak question:

> *"Lord, where should I go?"*

Or the common question:

> *"Lord, what should I do?"*

Or the only slightly better question:

> *"Lord, to whom should I go?"*

Is the reason we get such a poor response because it is difficult to give a good answer to a bad question?

I am convinced that the secret to the better question can be found in Abram's call.

> *"No longer will you be called Abram; your name will be Abraham, for I have made you a father of many nations."*[11]

God attached an initial from the divine name 'YHWH' to 'Abram,' making 'Abraham.'

That is significant!

By doing that, God was telling us something. Abraham's pilgrimage was intended to bind him to God. More specifically, it was intended to bind him to God's purposes. As he journeyed, the Father's dream would become his dream. God was not simply directing him to a geographical place, but through the journey, Abraham would begin to think, feel, and believe what God thinks, feels, and believes.

This is also where *you* are heading.

You see, there are better answers waiting for those who ask the better questions. There is a question that will lead to a better answer from God, because it is in line with the purpose of any pilgrimage to which He calls us.

So here is that better question:

> *What is the most effective thing I could do for God's Kingdom?*

This is the question I challenge people to ask when I bubble them. It is a question that has transformed the way I find God's will. It is the question we will explore throughout this book. It is also a question with a twist.

Ironically, as we seek first the Kingdom of God, something very strange happens. In Hebrew, the words God used when He told Abram to leave were:

> *Lekh lekha*

This Hebrew phrase literally means 'go,' but more specifically implies 'go to yourself.' Therefore, as one old rabbi observed in the Middle Ages, the Lord was saying:

> *You will gain from the journey. Lekha, to yourself, will be the benefit.*[12]

Seek first God's Kingdom, and you will stumble across your true self.

Brain

Abraham's pilgrimage was created to take him to a place where he would eventually have the mind of Christ. As wonderful as that idea is in itself, it comes with an additional bonus.

> *Do not conform to the pattern of this world, but be transformed by the renewing of your mind. Then you will be able to test and approve what God's will is—his good, pleasing and perfect will.*[13]

The Bible clearly teaches us that if our mind is transformed, then and only then will we be able to understand His will and direction for our lives. While current culture promotes going with your heart, God advises going with His mind.

The reason?

> *The heart is deceitful above all things . . .* [14]

Our words are the overflow of our hearts. Yet our hearts reflect who we like to think we are and what we like to think we want. Our hearts do not always tell us the truth. It doesn't surprise me that the message the 'prince of this world' promotes is that we choose our direction by what *feels* best. According to God's wisdom, our hearts are rarely in sync with our own actions, let alone God's! So only when our minds line up with His, will our search for His guidance gain more clarity than confusion.

But how exactly does that work?

Well, the spiritual dynamics parallel the biological ones. The reoccurring patterns in your brain are created by connections called synapses. These synapses connect the neurons in our brains and literally create a flow of thought. These biological pathways shape the way we think about everything!

Have you ever wondered who has the biggest brain in the room?

You may be surprised to learn it is the three year old. Oddly, the brain appears to grow backwards. It gets very big, very quickly, and then tightens or 'shrinks' back as you grow older.

Essentially, it becomes 'smaller' as you become smarter.

Forty-two days after you are conceived, your brain starts to experience a four-month growth spurt, starting with your first neuron, or brain cell. One hundred and twenty days later and you have a hundred billion of them. Sixty days before your birth, your neurons start communicating with each other, reaching out towards each other on a strand called an axon. A successful connection is called a synapse. At three years old, you have fifteen thousand connections for every one of your hundred billion neurons!

Then, your brain persuades you to ignore many of them!

Once disregarded, they fall into disrepair. By age sixteen, fifty percent of your network is gone! I guess you could say that at age sixteen you only have half a brain. No surprise, of course, to any parent of a teenager.

But why?

Why does your brain explode so quickly and then seem to ignore many avenues of thought? Well, your cleverness depends on how you capitalize on your strongest connections. Doing that depends on your ability to think clearly. A child's huge network that soaks up vital information eventually becomes just too much. Imagine having to choose between multiple options every time you think of the simplest daily action. You would be mentally hamstrung!

Therefore, you develop particular pathways of thought in order to make decisions more quickly and easily. This means that after a while certain ways of thinking begin to become more natural to you, partly because you are initially trained to think this way and partly because you later choose to do so. Your thoughts quite literally get into a rut of reacting almost exactly the same way to a complex amount of input.

Essentially, the more we think a certain way, the more we think *that* certain way.

Biologically, the stronger a particular thought pattern establishes itself, the harder another way of thinking becomes. If our thoughts are not already God's thoughts—and none of us are born that way—then can you imagine just how impossible it becomes for us to naturally think like Him?

This neurological reality creates a similar dynamic to the contrast between broadband and dial-up internet. Broadband is smooth and connectivity with various applications flows together with ease. Not so with the old dial-up connection. My dad, I am sure, was the last person in the universe with a dial-up modem. While the world was downloading videos, he was hanging around for three minutes longing for a photo to appear. Older readers might remember waiting for your computer to connect with the then mysterious internet. There would be a screeching noise and, if you were fortunate, after a few seconds the computer's modem seemed to hit the right spot and a connection would be made. Quite often, however, it would keep screeching, desperately trying to grasp hold of this invisible connection in the air.

Is this what is happening to you when one of God's thoughts drops into your brain?

If God's ways are your ways, then His flow of ideas finds it easy to stream into yours. If, however, you think along a different pattern than His, then it is like a struggling dial-up connection. You might get lucky, but even then, the connection can just as easily be dropped.

Although we have the potential of a broadband connection with God, many settle for dial-up.

Tupos

So is there any hope for us?

Are some of us just too old to be transformed? Has our ability to test and approve God's will dissipated? Could our minds be so conditioned by our upbringing, our past-thinking, and society that we can only grasp at spiritual straws when it comes to understanding His will?

No! There is good news!

The recent scientific discoveries of *neuroplasticity* have confirmed what the Bible has taught for two millennia. Our brains are not static as previously thought; our thinking can be rewired! In fact the Greek word *metamorphoō*, used to translate Paul's command to be transformed, is the root for the English word *metamorphosis.*[15]

A leopard may not be able to change its spots, but a pilgrim can change his or her pattern.

The secret?

Repetition.

Join with others in following my example, brothers, and take note of those who live according to the pattern we gave you.[16]

The Greek word used here for 'pattern' is a very interesting one.

Tupos: a die, stamp, scar; shape, something that is made by repeated blows[17]

Imagine you had a piece of corrugated cardboard like the flap of a cardboard box. The minute it bends you can see grooves, right? If you dropped some water onto that cardboard, it would automatically run down those grooves.

Now imagine you have a blunt knife and, with that instrument, you start to cut into the cardboard. The first slash is intended to cut a different groove going in a different direction from the others. The following strikes also go along that new path. Gradually these repeated blows (*tupos*) create a new groove, a new track, a new trail that is stronger and broader than the previous one. Eventually you reach a tipping point whereby, when you bend the cardboard again, it now bends in the form of least resistance . . . the new groove.

So it is with our thinking.

God uses patterns. He uses repeated blows, a repetitive stamping of His ways, so that we are eventually scarred by Him. Not in a negative way, but in a process whereby every time we exercise our thinking, the drops of thought run into *His* groove.

Think about the consequences of that!

Apparently, there is a courthouse in Ohio that stands in a unique location. Raindrops that fall on the north side of the building go into Lake Ontario and the Gulf of St. Lawrence, while those falling on the south side go into the Mississippi River and the Gulf of Mexico. At precisely the point of the peak of the roof, just a gentle puff of wind can determine the destiny of many raindrops. It will make a difference of more than 2,000 miles as to their destination.

So it is with our choices.

We all have made mistakes and, similar to using an old typewriter, we have had to use white-out and then redo. God, through His grace, has given us a similar opportunity—to make mistakes, ask for forgiveness, and be forgiven. However, we may still have to live with the consequences of those bad decisions. So, if there is one thing I suggest we can all agree on, it is this:

> It would be better to be shaped by the *tupos* of God than experience the *typos* of life.

6th

"I know what happens next."

That is the random thought that often rudely interrupts my mind when I sit down and listen to someone tell me their story. As they share the circumstances of their life, past and present, I suddenly realize I may know a little of their future. I don't mean in some kind of prophetic, mystic, crystal ball fashion. I mean in the same way experience teaches me what will happen next if I shake a can of soda and lift its pull-ring.

I have determined this is somewhat of a sixth sense I have, similar to that of the young boy from the Bruce Willis thriller, with one clear exception:

I don't see dead people. I see *patterns*.

They may be invisible to the naked eye, but they are very real. I believe that God uses these patterns to guide us.

> *Pattern: a plan or model used as a guide for making something.*[18]

God wants to make you significant, because you are already special. Patterns are God's way of developing you into a person who lives by faith and not by fate. They are His way of training you to know *why* He wants you to do something, not simply *what* He wants you to do.

Let me encourage you not to settle for anything less.

There have been times when people have helped me discover God's will by speaking words, inspired by God's Spirit, directly into my life. In some circles, this practice is described as 'prophecy' and has a significant but somewhat limited role in our ability to *consistently* know God's will and direction.

Prophecies give temporary answers to transient questions.

Prophecies provide special moments, but significant lives need more than just moments. They need processes. The problem is we love moments, don't we? We long for moments. The moment we are discovered. The moment everything turns around. The moment it all makes sense.

But could a longing for moments blind us to God's truest path?

Prophecies are just another form of circumstance. I believe in them just as much as I believe that God sends the wind and the rain. But they are often seasonal, circumstantial, and helpful for a moment in time. They may influence your next step, but they will not guarantee your future because your future is shaped by something else:

Your character.

In my mind at least, *patterns* trump *prophecies*. Prophecies don't shape you; patterns do.

It is important to note that patterns are like parables. Parables are designed to highlight a particular truth but are not fashioned to blend into each other. In the same way, the patterns operate independently of each other and are intended to highlight God's direction in our lives at certain times and in certain places because God uses each pattern to change our thinking in different ways. Therefore, one pattern may appear more applicable in one season of life and a different pattern will replace it in relevance at a later date.

Patterns are intended to reveal not only an alternative way of discovering God's direction, but also an *alternate reason for doing so.* This second benefit, of course, is the most important as we discover through this description of the pilgrim Abraham:

> *Finding his heart true to You, You made a covenant with him.*[19]

Covenant requires a true heart because only a true heart receives God's promises. So before we continue, let me ask you . . . What is in your heart? To get somewhere? To gain a position? To work with a certain person? To do something?

Or . . .

To have His thoughts become your thoughts? To see His ways become your ways? And to find His dreams become your dreams?

A pilgrim's journey is not about swapping *dreams.* It's about swapping *purposes.*

KINGDOM PATTERN

DIAMONDS

DIAMONDS | The Pattern

Simple

Growth is diamond-shaped.

When God plants a seed in our hearts, we immediately try to interpret what it may grow into. That is where we often make our first mistake. We attach what God has said to the nearest thing we know that looks like it. Then, connecting the two together, we paint a picture for ourselves that is hard to shake.

You see, the reason we miss God's direction in our lives is *not* because we do not know what it looks like, but because we have decided in advance what it looks like.

And then we make our second mistake:

We presume He will make it simple.

Subconsciously, we imagine a straightforward, narrow path to get us from our dreams to our destiny.

We expect a journey that equips us with the essential skills, experiences, and connections that we believe will help us make our dreams happen.

For instance, if you felt God gave you a vision about healing the sick, you might immediately decide he is calling you to be a doctor. You might then assume that the next step is to go to a nursing college and focus on medicine.

You may be correct . . . or you may be in for a surprise.

Short-cuts

Like you, King David was special, and also like you, he was chosen to be significant. The Psalmist himself tells God that:

> *You stoop down to make me great.*[20]

Yet notice what he also says:

> *You provide a broad path for my feet, so that my ankles do not give way.*[21]
> *You have made a wide path for my feet to keep them from slipping.*[22]
> *Thou hast enlarged my steps under me, that my feet did not slip.*[23]

I used to go fell walking and also mountain walking. Both require walking up energy-sapping slopes and yet they require a very different type of hiking boot. The first needs a supple boot, offering flexibility. The second requires a sturdier boot, offering more support because of the greater potential of misstepping, rolling an ankle, and walking the rest of the journey with a limp.

The first Kingdom Pattern that we will look at protects us from a similar fate.

God has thought ahead of time, specifically ahead of *your* time, to plan a path for you that strengthens your ankles and avoids the slip-ups that you might otherwise make.

Significantly, this particular Kingdom Pattern helps us avoid the blunders that are caused by something many of us go looking for . . .

Short-cuts.

There is a story of a barber shop in a small town that catered to the haircutting needs of its population. One day, a chain of hairdressers moved in and flooded the community with billboard advertisements that read:

Haircuts only $6! Hair coloring only $6! Perms only $6!

So, the local barber shop decided to call in a public relations expert. The consultant looked around at all the advertising billboards and suggested one strategy: to use the owner's life savings and rent the billboard directly above his barber shop. On it, the expert advised he put four simple words:

We fix $6 haircuts.

It was a stroke of genius. Those four words struck a chord with passersby. They resonated with the gut instinct we all have. The gut instinct that tells us that short-cuts are rarely healthy and, in the long-term, often get us lost.

And so it is with this Kingdom Pattern.

It helps us understand the purpose of a longer journey.

Long-Johns

This diamond-shaped Kingdom Pattern seems counter-intuitive.

When God calls us, He initially *broadens* our path. This is confusing because God can give us a vision and then appear to immediately direct us away from it!

After revealing His dream, God will begin to lead you into many other experiences that at first appear to have nothing to do with what He has just said to you. In fact, not only do they have little in common with the dream, these experiences tend to have little in common with each other!

I have seen this broadening of my path many times in my life.

The first came when I finished school. I had no vision for my career, so I said yes to the first thing I was offered. It was an apprenticeship in retail management with the Co-Op, the largest retailer in the UK at the time. I was given a choice to work in their food or non-food departments, and I chose non-food. However, the Co-Op immediately shipped me out to every conceivable type of retail store under the sun. At age seventeen, I sold carpets, cutlery, oranges, garden sheds, lamb cutlets, televisions, holidays, and long-johns. I traveled to huge superstores and tiny corner shops with the assignment of managing them while the head of the department was on vacation or sick. I worked in a butcher shop, garden center, department store, farmers' market, and a wide variety of other retail outlets throughout Greater Manchester. All of these experiences taught me things that I did not realize I would need to know later. The initial broadening of my path had a dual purpose; it taught me practical lessons for that time, but also a greater spiritual lesson for the years to come.

Even though I was not following God for some of that time, it was all part of His plan.

Each facet of that apprenticeship taught me things I would need to know when leading an international missionary organization. Directing Pais would require dealing with people from all walks of life, and my retail itinerary was the best possible training for gathering people together to work for a common purpose. As a skinny, spotty teenager with a blazer two sizes too big, every few weeks I would walk into a different store to manage staff three times my age. It was my job to motivate people to sell products of which I had little to no knowledge but they were experts in. I quickly needed to develop people skills in order to inspire them to respect me. I had to learn organizational skills when the staff came to me with vacation requests, discipline issues, and team conflicts. The challenges were huge, and so were the lessons learned.

The second major broadening of my path came with my calling.

Six years after my baptism by fire in retail management, I had a sense that God was leading me to be a missionary. I went to Scotland for a short course in evangelism and discipleship, expecting to then be sent to Africa, Papua New Guinea, or somewhere exotic and desperate. Surprisingly, however, I felt led to return to Manchester[24] and there I offered myself in a voluntary capacity to work for my church. The next season in my life involved visiting the elderly, praying for the sick, listening to my pastor's experiences, completing office tasks, fixing things, creating memos from my denomination's business meetings, and helping to draw up a new trust deed and constitution for our church.

The work was sometimes boring, often disconnected, and when compared to the things I felt God had laid upon my heart, they made no sense at all.

Ever been in that position yourself?

At first the way of the diamond can be confusing, deflating, and appear distracting. Yet it is God's way of preparing you. Not preparing you for what you *think* the vision will be, but preparing you for what He really has in mind:

> *The joining of your dream to His.*

It equips you *now* with all the things you don't realize you will need *then*.

Hinges

Four years after returning to Manchester, something strange happened. Visionary inversion.

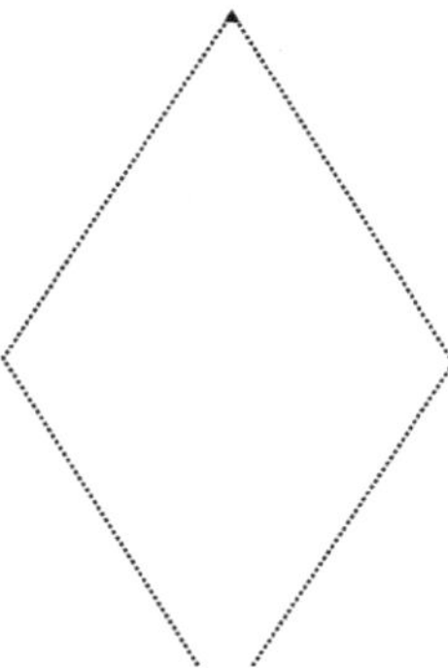

After God broadens your path, He begins to narrow your focus and energy. Gradually, the pointless experiences you have accumulated begin to connect, to fit . . . *to help.*

Things start to come into focus.

When I was first given my seed of vision, I interpreted it to mean that I might be a missionary in Africa, and the experiences that then followed seemed to hamper my progress. But when I realized I was being called to pioneer a missionary organization, the lessons became clear.

The countless visits to the old folk had taught me, a young man, how to relate to those who would host Pais apprentices and financially support the work of the vision in those early days. Long, dull business meetings provided insight into the legal issues and principles I would face when we set up charities in various nations. The endless reams of notes from the ministers' fraternal gave me the precious insight into church leadership mentality which became vital when creating partnerships with congregations from various denominations.

My broader skills equaled better solutions!

You see, if the only tool you have is a hammer, you will see every problem as a nail.

The narrow dotted path, like a heavy hammer, will lead you somewhere fast and furious. If God's plan is no more than a vision to do something special in a certain place, then that is the path He would set out for you. The diamond, however, shapes you to be confident and curious *because* God's plan for you is to become someone strategic everywhere you go.

This broadening of your path, this diamond-shaped journey, will do two things for you.

Firstly, it will filter out what you thought God meant and factor in what He really had in mind. Simply put, it will keep you from being narrow-minded when interpreting God's directions for your life. It prevents you from jumping to conclusions and taking a leap of faith onto the wrong path.

Secondly, you will gain a sharpness of vision with a breadth of experience. At the upper end of the diamond, you will spend most of your time doing the things that only you should do. You will be used more strategically. In the early days of leading Pais, I did everything, but now I mainly do the things that are most effective for me to do. The DNA of my responsibilities fit much more in line with the purpose I was given. I am now fulfilling the dream but in a way that I had not imagined. I have been trained in ways I never knew I needed because God's need of me is bigger than I knew.

You see, diamonds exist because vision is best approached as a theme, not a target.

I thought I would be a missionary.

Instead I make missionaries.

Discussion starters

1. Put a circle around where you consider yourself to be in this Kingdom Pattern.
2. Please write down your explanation for this.
3. Is there somewhere else you would prefer to be? If so place an 'X' to mark the spot.
4. Is there an additional principle you see in the pattern that is not stated in the book?
5. Please share your thoughts on social media using: #kingdompatterns

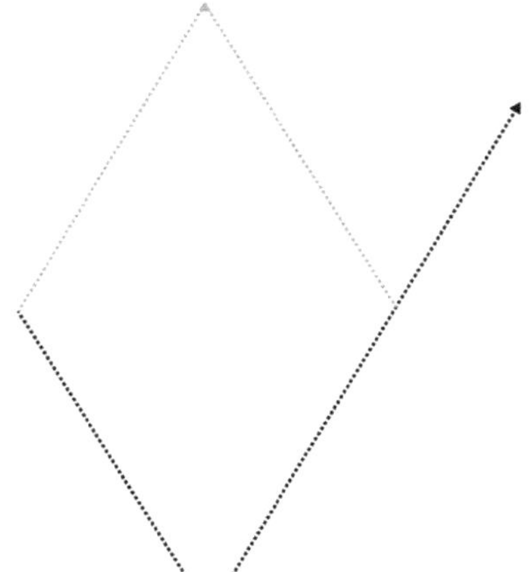

DIAMONDS | The Pilgrim

Joseph

There is so much we can learn from those who have gone before us.

> *Do you see what this means—all these pioneers who blazed the way, all these veterans cheering us on? It means we'd better get on with it. Strip down, start running—and never quit!*[25]

One such veteran is Joseph, whose life is a perfect example of diamond-shaped growth. His story started with a dream, a seed sown into his heart and mind while he was asleep, which he then shared with his father and brothers.[26]

> *He said to them, "Listen to this dream I had: We were binding sheaves of grain out in the field when suddenly my sheaf rose and stood upright, while your sheaves gathered around mine and bowed down to it."*[27]

In actual fact, he had two dreams; both seemed to imply that one day his family would submit themselves to him. He obviously expected his kinsfolk to receive this revelation with delight. I even wonder if he naively expected them to crown him there and then. Either way, I am certain that he figured God would make his path straight.

But, no. The next thing that happened to him was that he was sold into slavery!

> *Joseph's brothers pulled him out of the cistern and sold him to them for twenty pieces of silver. And the traders took him to Egypt.*[28]

Immediately, his life seemed to go the very opposite way of his dream! Eventually his journey led to him being bought as a slave by Potiphar, an officer to Pharaoh.[29] Yet, importantly, God prospered him as he served his new master well.

> *The Lord was with Joseph, so he succeeded in everything he did as he served in the home of his Egyptian master.*[30]

However, I bet he did not *feel* like God was with him!

At this point in his life, I wonder what Joseph presumed was happening. Perhaps he began to believe that his dream had little to do with his family and everything to do with Potiphar's household instead. However, just as he was beginning to settle into his role and see some success, an even more devastating blow presented itself. Potiphar's wife attempted to seduce Joseph and because he refused her, she accused him of attempted rape.[31]

> *Potiphar was furious when he heard his wife's story about how Joseph had treated her. So he took Joseph and threw him into the prison where the king's prisoners were held, and there he remained.*[32]

Joseph is clearly in the bottom half of the diamond of growth, apparently moving further and further *away* from the vision he had received.

How desperate he must have felt . . .

How very alone!

How very forgotten!

How very confused!

In prison, however, he was again given responsibility and God blessed him in it.[33] Then another peculiar turn of events occurred. He was asked to interpret the dreams of two fellow inmates, a cup-bearer and a baker. Just as Joseph predicted, the baker died and the cup-bearer was restored into the service of Pharaoh.[34]

Great! Not only did Joseph get it right, but the cup-bearer promised that he would remember Joseph and help him get out of jail. Yet for many more years, Joseph remained in prison as the cup-bearer forgot the promise he made. I cannot even imagine the misery and heartache that Joseph must have felt during that time. Yet, often when things are at their bleakest . . .

Inversion happens.

Out of the blue, the cup-bearer remembered Joseph and he was summoned to interpret the Pharaoh's dreams. After listening to the king, he predicted seven years of plenty followed by seven years of severe famine. Even though his prediction could not be tested, Joseph's credibility gave the king confidence in him. The not-so-young dreamer was suddenly promoted to become Pharaoh's right-hand man.[35]

> *So Joseph took charge of the entire land of Egypt.*[36]

Over the following years, Joseph approached the apex of his diamond and therefore did less and less of the things that were not essential to his calling. He was given servants and staff so that he could spend more and more of his time on what most effectively advanced God's purposes. During that time, Joseph managed the storing and then sharing of Egyptian food and effectively saved his people from eradication by starvation!

His diamond not only inverted, but narrowed to a piercing sharpness.

The Book of Genesis then tells us the rest of the story. It is a complex tale well worth a read and full of twists and turns. Spoiler alert: it

is the story of how Joseph's family came to Egypt and literally fell before Joseph, begging him for help.

Joseph's dream was realized.

Yet when it first budded, it did not look like, feel like, or taste like what he had imagined. It was much bigger, much better, and, importantly, at the right time . . . Joseph was ready for it!

Natural

Sometimes, the Bible makes short note of what must have been a complex process. The jump from recognizing someone has the ability to interpret your dream to believing they have the capacity to run your nation is a huge leap. I am convinced, therefore, that Pharaoh not only saw Joseph's *supernatural* ability but was influenced by his *natural* ability as well.

Joseph had grown through his diamond-shaped life. No matter how disappointed, how disillusioned, and how disconnected he felt, he never allowed it to impact his faithfulness in what God put before him. In fact, those experiences bound him closer to a God who would use him to rescue his people, because *his* dreams died and *God's* dream came more into focus. This bonding of his character to God's was key to successfully walking the diamond.

As a young man, Joseph showed the kind of responsibility that made him useful to his father. He ran errands and completed chores in such a way that he earned paternal love and the famous coat of many colors. His small duties, faithfully completed within his family, also gave him the skills to manage Potiphar's household. That responsibility in turn empowered him with the experience to manage a governmental institution. At each stage his commitment to excellence was developed and enhanced.

Then one day . . .

> *Pharaoh said to Joseph, "I hereby put you in charge of the entire land of Egypt."*[37]

Within the memo-like brevity of verse forty-one, we see the fruit of a seed that Joseph never allowed to be crushed. Pharaoh had not only experienced Joseph's mystical gifting, but would certainly have seen the track record in administration that the man who stood before him had built over many years.

What had grown under the surface, gaining nutrients from wherever they could be found, broke the surface and grew to dizzy heights.

Supernatural

The diamond of growth, however, is an opportunity to grow in more ways than one.

Not only had God stooped down and prepared Joseph in a natural way so that when his moment came his ankle would not turn, but He was also training him supernaturally.

Historical context is important for us to fully understand Joseph's story. You see, in Joseph's day, a far greater significance was put on dreams. If someone had a divine visitation while they were sleeping, then the place in which they lay became a holy site.[38] Manuals that explained how to interpret dreams were both popular and expensive. If someone had a problem and needed direction from the gods, they might visit an oracle or spend a night sleeping at a temple, believing that their god was more likely to give them a dream in a holy place.

It has also been recorded that in those days there were categories of dreams, each with a different level of interpretation and each giving a different level of status to those who interpreted them.[39] The explanation of these categories reveals another facet of Joseph's diamond-shaped journey.

First, there were '*simple message dreams*.'

These visions were straightforward and obvious; there was no need for any interpretation as the dreamer could understand them immediately.

At a second level there were '*simple symbolic dreams*.'

Not as clear as the first type, they involved elements or metaphors, yet they would still, after some meditation, make sense to the one who dreamt them.

Coming in at the third level were '*complex symbolic dreams*.'

Although still involving ciphers and icons, there was an important and profound difference with this kind of imagery. These types of dreams could not be interpreted by the dreamer but instead required others, usually a specialist, to decipher them. People made a very good career from interpreting this level of dream.

The final and loftiest dream category is what I call a '*royal complex dream*.'

Again, this was a message that needed interpretation but, significantly, it was had by someone in authority. What marked this dream out from any other was that it was considered to not affect just the dreamer, but to impact everyone under their leadership.

So when we retrace the Kingdom Pattern in Joseph's life, it does not require a brain surgeon to interpret what was going on. As he walked the diamond, he was gaining spiritual insight. There is no record of Joseph having a dream before the one mentioned in his story, but note that his brothers refer to him as 'that dreamer.'[40] It is possible that this refers to either the dream we know of, or an indication that he already had a reputation for dreaming. Either way, we see a spiritual progression because what he shares with his brothers is a *simple symbolic* dream, yet by the time that Pharaoh's cupbearer and baker seek his advice, Joseph had become a specialist in *complex symbolic dreams*.[41] The king's servants were getting the benefit of a man who was growing in a mystical art that God was not only endorsing, but also anointing him in.

Then, Pharaoh brought to our young hero the highest level of dream, a *royal complex dream*, and it was effortlessly interpreted.[42]

In both the natural and supernatural realms, Joseph benefited from a path that was broadened by God. Joseph's life did not change on a dime or a whim of Pharaoh. Although there was a moment where everything *seemed* to have changed, in reality the change had been ongoing for years.

Whenever his moment came, Joseph did not need to *try*; he had been *trained*.

Discussion starters

Please take a look at these incidents from Joseph's life. Then put the number for each one where you think he was on this Kingdom Pattern.

1. Joseph receives his dream: Genesis 37:5
2. Joseph in Potiphar's home: Genesis 39:2
3. Joseph is thrown into prison: Genesis 39:19-20
4. Joseph interprets Pharaoh's dream: Genesis 41
5. Joseph settles his family in Egypt: Genesis 47:12

What is a key principle you see in Joseph's diamond-shaped journey?

Please share the principle on social media using: #kingdompatterns

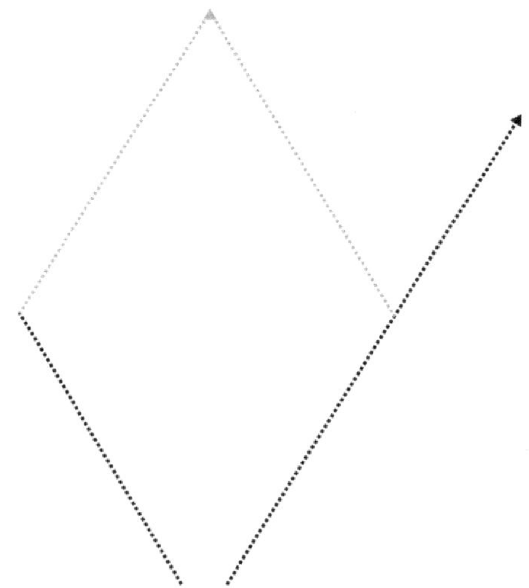

DIAMONDS | The Practices

Colt

Practice #1: *Recognize a seed for what it is!*

It is important. It is significant. It is the vision.

The lower half of the diamond is just as much part of the vision as the tip. Please understand that the whole of the diamond is God's vision for your life. God is binding you to Him all along the way.

Joseph was sixteen years old when he was first given his dream. He was thirty years old when it 'came true.' That was fourteen long years of walking the diamond, but *not* fourteen years of waiting for the vision to become true. It was fourteen years of practicing its truth. Remember, God's dream for you is not to get you to a place or position but to tie you to His purpose, and that will happen *all along* the path.

Many years ago, a woman said that God had given her a vision to share with me. In it, she saw a young colt only a few months old, tied to a fence in a small pen. It was anxious and agitated as it looked out into the next field where the 'big horses' were playing. Even as she was talking, the message was immediately clear to me and completely relevant to how I was feeling. With a head full of heroes and a mind that could retell the biography of some of the most famous

modern missionaries, I was desperate to get out there and be one of them. I wanted to run with the big horses.

She continued on, explaining how this little horse was doing everything it could to pull, tear, and gnaw at the rope that was holding it down. It needed to be patient, because if it succeeded and jumped the fence, it would get hurt by the animals much bigger than itself.

Yes, I had so much to learn, but importantly, I had so many people that I needed to serve. The years at the Co-op and assisting my pastor were not years of treading water. They were just as important as the journey I am on now. The Kingdom Pattern is a challenge to be the best you can be for God every step of the way, not simply when you arrive.

God is not giving you a target to get to, but a theme to live by . . . *everywhere* and *every when.*

Sharpie

Practice #2: *Force an opportunity and you'll spoil a future possibility!*

Be patient. Be prepared. Be productive on the way.

When God gives you a dream, it is simply a declaration of intent. When I teach this Kingdom Pattern, I show a photograph of an infant and a toddler. The toddler has a big smile on his face, grasping a Sharpie pen in his hand and two arms raised in victory. He is obviously celebrating his achievement and taking credit for his work of art. Asleep next to him is his baby sister, covered from head to toe in colored doodles.

God will never give an immature disciple a spiritual Sharpie.

Why?

He knows that if we are given a significant opportunity too soon, we may not only make a mess but also ruin our future prospects.

Modern Christians have a tendency to do that, don't we? And we are not the only ones. Some commentators believe that Joseph's sharing of his dream was his way of attempting to make it happen.

> *When he told his father as well as his brothers, his father rebuked him and said, "What is this dream you had? Will your mother and I and your brothers actually come and bow down to the ground before you?"*[43]

I know from experience that I forced certain opportunities too early. For instance, I was not ready for certain speaking opportunities I created when I was younger. Twenty years later, I expect that some people still remember me at the level of skill I was then and may not feel confident giving me those opportunities again.

Don't grasp for something now that God intends to hand to you later.

Essence

Practice #3: *Never lose sight of what you have seen!*

Define it. Devote yourself to it. Don't be dissuaded from it.

The problem with the diamond is that this path can last a long time, and while you are on it, you can begin to lose sight of the true dream that God planted within you. As it begins to fade, a *pseudo-dream* can start to take its place.

Perhaps you think you heard God wrong?

Or maybe you feel God just forgot?

When this happens, we tend to replace the principles of the dream with an expansion of the tangible things we are presently doing.

We must be careful not to give up on the *essence* of what God told us and replace it with an *example* of what He might have meant.

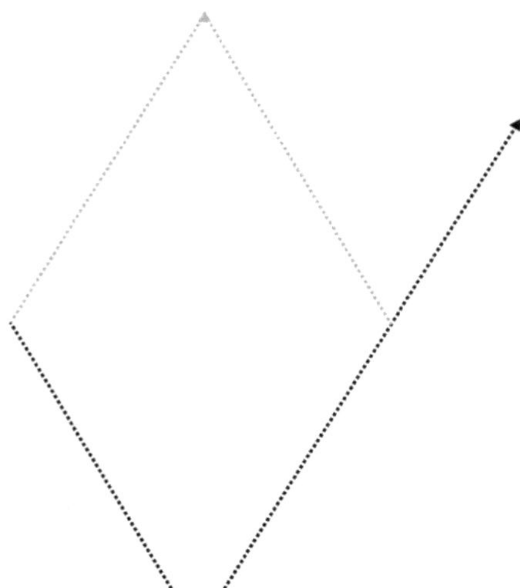

How do we know when we are doing this? When we no longer ask, "What is the most effective thing I could do for His Kingdom?" But instead we find ourselves asking, "What is the quickest way I can get to my dream?"

Abraham, our fellow pilgrim, made a similar mistake after he was given his theme.

> *". . . for I have made you a father of many nations."*

He lost the essence of *"for I"* and replaced it with an example of how he imagined it. He expected it to happen a certain way and when it took longer than he hoped, he looked for God's direction amongst his friends and family.

> *Now Sarai, Abram's wife, had not been able to bear children for him. But she had an Egyptian servant named Hagar. So Sarai said to Abram, "The Lord has prevented me from having children. Go and sleep with my servant. Perhaps I can have children through her." And Abram agreed with Sarai's proposal.*[44]

Abraham's shortcut created two brothers, two nations that have been opposing each other for centuries: the Jew and the Arab.

Please don't replace what you know God said with what you hope He meant.

Rivets

Practice #4: *Realize that one diamond may reside within another!*

Believe in it. Bargain on it. Be emboldened by it.

In ages past, it was widely known that the best way to cut a diamond was with another diamond. God still seems to think that's the best method, and so, your life may in fact look like one big diamond made up of several smaller ones.

God intends for us to be grown through repetition, each diamond slowly and surely forcing us to absorb the qualities we need to fulfill His dream while chipping away at dreams we have that miss His point.

This process takes a long time, perhaps even a lifetime. Therefore, it is good to remember that God's promises are like Sydney Harbor Bridge, one of Australia's greatest engineering feats that spans the city's business district and the North Shore. An iconic image of its nation, the bridge was opened in 1932 and was listed as the world's widest long-span bridge in the *Guinness World Records* until 2012. It has held various records, yet perhaps one of its more profound structural elements is that it only contains *sixteen* nuts and bolts.

The bridge is held together almost completely by six million rivets!

Why? Well, when this bridge was designed, it was never meant to be dismantled. The same can be said of God's promises. They span from the moment a dream is given to the moment it is fulfilled. Yet it may take more than one diamond to fully build the vision God has for you. So acknowledging that a particular dream may be part of something much bigger than you will allow you to wrap your life around something more substantial than you.

Remember, shortcuts bring only momentary gains . . . but diamonds are forever!

Award

Practice #5: *Look for the hints in your history!*

Embrace them. Engage with them. Be educated by them.

Your history shapes you for what lies ahead.

In the second book of this series, I shared about my mother's tenacity and her stubborn determination to work on my behalf and get me into the school of her dreams.[45] It's an odd story that many people have commented on. Yet, there was another side to her, the side that seemed to do the opposite of growing me but was just a different way of achieving the same goal.

I started work at twelve years old and I've not stopped since. Along with my father, my mother encouraged me to get a job when I was young. I worked for a local carpet shop delivering newsletters around the area. At age thirteen I became a golf caddy. I hated it. Every Saturday and Sunday when other kids were playing, I pulled a golf cart for four hours each day with a golf bag that pretty much equaled my body weight. It took me an hour to get to the golf course and an hour to get home. I was only paid one pound sterling per day and it cost me ten pence for a Mars bar to keep me going. That's a 90 pence profit for six hours of work.[46]

When I became a Christian, I was truly 'saved' because going to church on Sundays meant that I didn't have to caddy. However, I had no chance of stopping work. My mother took me to a local co-op supermarket and I was employed on Thursday nights, the occasional Friday night, and all day Saturday. She had an agenda and it involved me "knowing the value of money."

I remember my first trip to the city center on my own as a young boy. I've always been a little dizzy, and although I never got lost, I did lose most of my bus fare home. I called my mother to ask if I could be picked up but she refused. Instead of "Doris' taxi service," I would need to "be creative." So I bought a sealed packet of six post cards for the few pence I still had in my pocket, unwrapped them, and sold them individually on the streets until I had enough money to return home.

Pais has benefited from the lessons I learned about stewardship from my parents. We have always had a reputation with our financial supporters for making their pennies go a very long way. We also have a reputation for empowering others and bringing out the potential in them. Some of the techniques we use to do this, I read in books or learned from others. But many, without a doubt the more important ones . . . I just grew up with.

In my mid-twenties, my mother died of cancer. She had worked as a nurse most of her life, but for the last few years she served at a school for physically and mentally handicapped children. A few months after her funeral, my dad and I were asked to attend the school's annual award ceremony. It was the first year they were to give out what would become the annual Doris Gibbs Award. Before they announced the winner, one of the teachers stood up and began to remind everybody of Doris' legendary "philosophy on life."

What philosophy on life?!!

I sat there proud but more than a little bemused. This was all news to me! We were told of how Doris Gibbs championed an emphasis on self-sufficiency and resourcefulness, specifically how she encouraged the empowerment of students to become more independent. That day, the prize given in her memory went to a child who could not dress himself at the beginning of the school year but was able to do so by its end. Doris Gibbs, we were told, would have loved that. Every year since, the school dedicates the victory of a child's independence to her memory.

Sometimes our past can feel like a riddle; sometimes we are even encouraged to leave the past in the past. Should we? God, it seems, works all things in our history for the good of the future of those who love Him.

God loves us and trains us because He knows something of our future, and mysteriously it seems, so did my mum. When I was a young boy, I asked her why I was given the middle name Clayton, as it seemed a bit fancy for a boy from North Manchester. She told me it was in case I was ever on stage . . . or wrote a book.[47]

History. It's a clue.

Discussion starters

Practice #1: *Recognize a seed for what it is!*
Practice #2: *Force an opportunity and you'll spoil a future possibility!*
Practice #3: *Never lose sight of what you have seen!*
Practice #4: *Realize that one diamond may reside within another!*
Practice #5: *Look for the hints in your history!*

1. Which of these practices seems most relevant to you at this point in your journey?
2. What is the next practical step for you to take?
3. What questions do you still have?
4. What advice that I have not written would you give someone journeying on this pattern?
5. Please share your advice and questions on social media using: #kingdompatterns

KINGDOM PATTERN

SUMMITS

SUMMITS | The Pattern

Depth

Faith is summit-shaped.

When God shows us a dream, we are often inspired by those who realized theirs. In that moment, a temptation can creep in: we want to be where our heroes are, but we do not want to walk the path that got them there.

We may not even understand it.

Why? Because we may not fully understand the primary purpose of faith.

From a very young age, Joel, my eldest son, stopped hugging me. He was just too busy! He never stopped for a cuddle, and so I had to invent ways of making it happen. For instance, I would take him to the swimming pool and carry him into the shallow end. He would splash, play, and generally mess around. Slowly, I would take him that little bit deeper to where the water covered his ankles, then his knees, then his waist, and eventually up to his chest. At some point, Joel would realize we were moving towards the deep end, and he would start to grab hold of me, nervously laughing as he gripped my shoulders tighter and tighter, eventually wrapping himself completely around me. He sensed he was in more danger in the deep end than he had been in the shallow end.

He was, of course, wrong.

Because he had not yet learned to swim, he was at as much risk of drowning in three feet of water as he was in six feet. The depth did not change his need of me . . .

It just made him more *aware* of it.

At Pais, most of us 'live by faith.' That is the common term used by others for those with no guaranteed salary, those who have 'stepped out in faith' and voluntarily live off the generous financial support of those who give to the cause as and when they can. One month there is money; another month there may not be. Yet this idea of us distinctly living by faith is misleading; it suggests that others do not have to.

You may have been to college, have great qualifications, and have a secure job, but you are living by faith just as much as we are. Our income may depend on the month to month voluntary giving to Pais, but we are in no more danger of financial failure than you are. We need faith no more than you do. The financial ups and downs we face do not change our need for faith . . .

They simply make us a little more aware of it.

So why is the idea so common that only certain people 'live by faith'? Could it be because we think of faith primarily as that which is keeping us spiritually afloat? It is as though we think faith is intended only to help us believe that bad things won't happen and that we can get through them if they do.

Yet faith that pleases God is not a matter of personal survival but of Kingdom synergy!

Thankfully, there is a Kingdom Pattern for that.

Success

The Psalmist, thanking God for lifting him out of the depths and then raising him to dizzy heights, uses some peculiar language.[48]

> *When things were going great I crowed, "I've got it made. I'm God's favorite. He made me king of the mountain." Then you looked the other way and I fell to pieces.*[49]

God wants you to increase in your faith, but He has a strange way of showing it. You might think, for instance, that the journey of increasing faith happens in a straight line.

Surely faith breeds success, which breeds greater faith, right?

If that is the case, then God should immediately reward our acts of faithfulness in order to encourage us that faith works. The intended path of faith would therefore take us from one success straight to another in constant perpetuation.

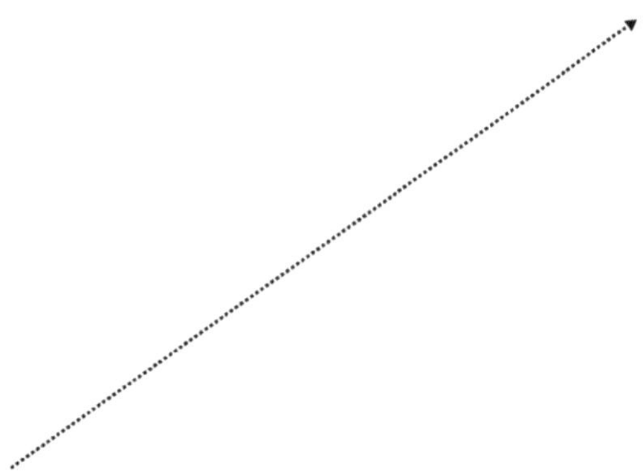

For instance, if you're a pastor, ever increasing faith would mean that every single week a few extra people attend your church, encouraging you to plan for bigger attendance. If you're a business owner, ever increasing faith would mean that every month your profits increase so you can consistently fund God's work to a greater degree. If you're a follower of Jesus, ever increasing faith would mean that every day you feel a little holier or spiritually stronger than the day before, giving us more and more encouragement to follow Him in the future.

Surely this is the plan, isn't it?

Well, no. In reality, faith is a zig zag of highs and lows.

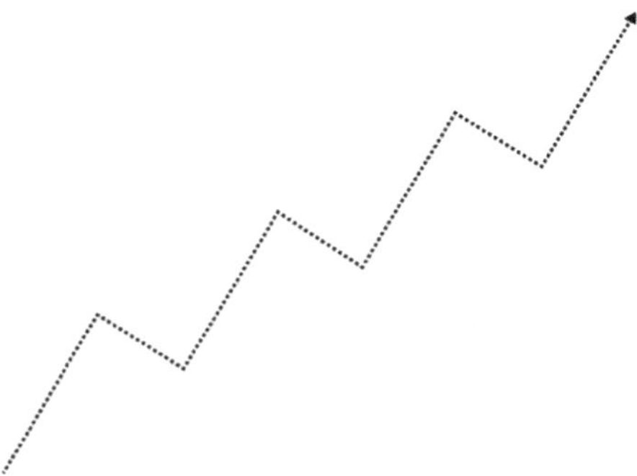

In the Kingdom of God, faith does not come by a collection of consistent achievements. It follows a path that is intentionally erratic. It is purposely planned to encourage but then humble us, and it does this for a peculiar reason.

God lifts us up, giving us gifts of faith to believe Him for things we *think* He wants to do. Then, in that moment of triumph, He will often show us we spent a long time climbing a ladder of faith only to find it was leaning against the wrong wall.

This Kingdom Pattern acts as a spiritual exercise machine. God takes us through a series of highs and lows in order to shape, break, and then re-shape our dreams. He does this not simply so our dreams come into line with His, but so that His dreams *become* ours.

As the saying goes:

> *If you want to test a man make him a failure, but if you want to really test a man make him a success.*[50]

God does not test us in order to find something out about us. He is omniscient and knows us completely already. He tests us so we can find things out about ourselves . . . and Him.

Before I unpack this more, let me just say that the idea of mountaintop and valley experiences are of course an old concept in Christianity. This Kingdom Pattern, however, is not the path of *incidental* growth where we simply learn to hold onto God when things go wrong. How shortsighted that would be! If all we do is grow in our valley experiences, then we will let go of God on our mountaintops. No. This is the path of *intentional* growth, because . . .

Faith that is grown on a mountaintop is greater than that which is grown in a valley.

False

The truth about faith is this:

Faith is a moving target.

I was in my early twenties when I climbed my first mountain. It was in Scotland and I was excited because I had never seen anything like it before. As soon as I saw its peak from the road, I wanted to be on top of it. There was a group of us and I remember running ahead of everyone else, eager to reach the summit first. I arrived before the others, exhausted but victorious, and wondered why everyone else was taking so long. Then I looked up and suddenly realized that what I thought was the peak, was in reality only the cusp of a plateau and the true mountaintop was ten times further than I initially thought.

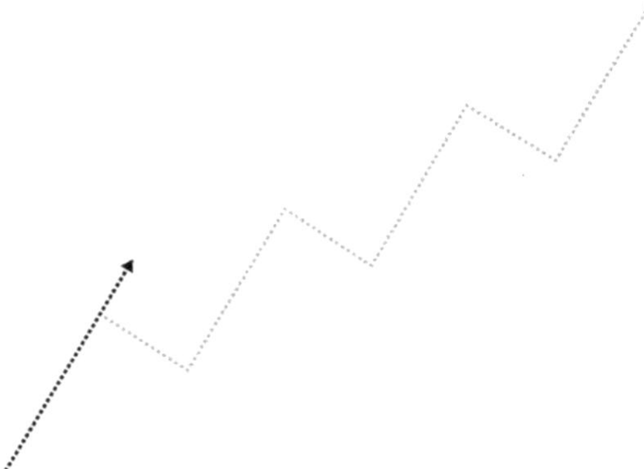

When God gives us vision, all we ever really see are false summits.

From a long distance, you may be able to see the zenith of the vision. Hazy, blurry, but with enough beauty to inspire you to set out on the climb. However, at the base of the mountain and during most of the climb, your line of sight is disabling. It can hide from view everything that lies behind that first peak . . . or first peek.

God is sneaky.

And He is sneaky for a reason.

Discussion starters

1. Put a circle around where you consider yourself to be in this Kingdom Pattern.
2. Please write down your explanation for this.
3. Is there somewhere else you would prefer to be? If so place an 'X' to mark the spot.
4. Is there an additional principle you see in the pattern that is not stated in the book?
5. Please share your thoughts on social media using: #kingdompatterns

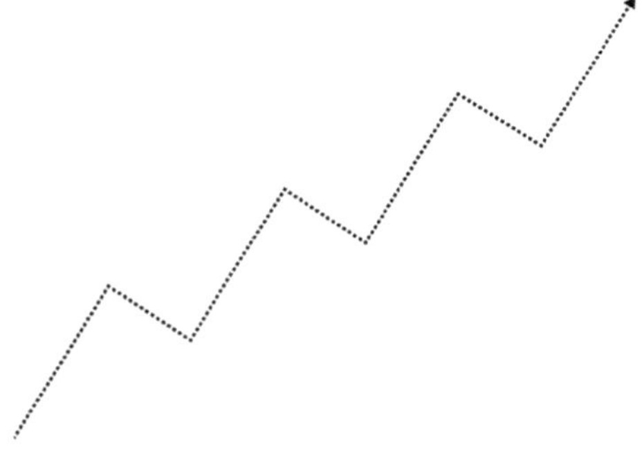

SUMMITS | The Pilgrim

Peter

Faith is shaped best when we walk on a path not of highs and highs, but of highs and lows with one important dynamic—the highs get higher and the lows are not quite as low as they used to be.

Perhaps no man in history exemplifies this Kingdom Pattern better than Peter. So to explain this dynamic and the purpose of our summit-shaped journey, let me choose one of his false summits:

> *The next day, the news that Jesus was on the way to Jerusalem swept through the city. A large crowd of Passover visitors took palm branches and went down the road to meet him. They shouted, "Praise God! Blessings on the one who comes in the name of the Lord! Hail to the King of Israel!"*[51]

How must Peter have felt when walking alongside Jesus during that triumphal entry? Elated? Fulfilled? Excited? Vindicated? Proud?

After almost three years of serving Jesus and putting his faith in this miracle-working revolutionary, surely this was it! He was now about to see his ultimate success. Jesus would be crowned, a new kingdom would be established, and Peter was going to have a prominent role in it all! However, five days after the triumphal entry:

Peter had denied Jesus.

Peter was alone.

Peter was at rock bottom.

Or was he?

Although Peter betrayed Jesus on the eve of Christ's crucifixion, he was actually much closer to understanding Jesus' purpose for his life than when he caught the miraculous catch of fish or even walked on water. He was beginning to understand Jesus' true dream rather than impose his own expectations on the Messiah.

But why did his path need to take him through so many ups and downs?

Well, first we need to understand who Peter was and what he was hoping for.

He started as a fisherman. In fact, many of Jesus' disciples did, which was odd. The Jews were fearful of large expanses of water, which they called the 'abyss.' They believed them to contain evil spirits, therefore the profession of fishing was rare amongst Jews. The fact that Jesus chose fishermen as five of His twelve closest companions was a statement in itself. These were men who dared to live their lives on the edge of the abyss, willing to risk physical and spiritual danger in order to harvest its rewards.

Peter was not a zealot but he was certainly from an area that grew them. The north coast of the Sea of Galilee was a hot-bed for hot-heads. It hosted those most passionate about bringing in a new government, one that would make them subjects of God and not of Rome. It was an area that encouraged the kind of extremists and revolutionaries who would give their lives for their beliefs and, sadly, take their own lives for them as well.[52] Peter had that revolutionary blood flowing through him and his mind thought in similar ways. He was looking for a hero to usher in a new kingdom, and he expected some kind of revolution or rebellion to bring it about.

So Peter's initial faith was in a victory that he could understand and be excited about. Up until Jesus' death and resurrection, Peter displayed great imagination. He could see his hero ushering in a new kingdom. He had the faith to believe in it, *but* he lacked two things.

Firstly, he did not have in mind the kind of kingdom that Jesus had in mind!

Secondly, he never imagined it appearing the way Jesus knew it would.

Jesus' vision would not require domination; it would require submission. The mature faith Peter would need in order to act as a catalyst and pillar in the early Church would require him to understand and become excited about *that* vision.

Peter's pilgrimage was designed to *bind* his faith to God's, and so is yours! His summit-shaped journey changed his way of thinking, and as his thinking transformed, so did his ability to know God's will.

God's sneakiness aims to separate us from our purposes and lead us towards His by allowing us to walk up our summit only to see that, when compared to God's purposes, it is no summit at all.

You see, following Christ is not simply about having faith for following Jesus.

It is about having faith for the things that Jesus has faith for.

Quasi

I have never been arrested.

I have been chased through a Berlin subway by the German police for 'breaking' an underground train. I have been water-hosed by officials for sleeping overnight in a zoo. I have been banned from two parts of the world and twice frog-marched by armed police out of high security areas. I have been interrogated by the police after a drug party at my flat. I have been stopped, frisked, and spread eagled against a fence due to mistaken identity. Oh, and I was once barred from a pub that I had never even entered for unruly behavior while in the pub. (It's complicated.)

But I have never been arrested.

God was, though.

God was chained and forced to go where He did not want to go. Paradoxically, He allowed it to happen. In fact, He knew it would happen.

And Peter went with Him . . . to a point.

> *Simon Peter followed Jesus, as did another of the disciples. That other disciple was acquainted with the high priest, so he was allowed to enter the high priest's courtyard with Jesus. Peter had to stay outside the gate. The disciple who knew the high priest spoke to the woman watching at the gate, and she let Peter in.*[53]

Through a friend of a friend, Peter was able to get close to his beloved Jesus, but he was just outside of the room where Jesus was put on trial.

So near, yet so far!

Or so it seemed.

> *Meanwhile, as Simon Peter was standing by the fire warming himself, they asked him again, "You're not one of his disciples, are you?" He denied it, saying, "No, I am not."*[54]

While Peter was disassociating himself from his Lord, the High Priest was asking Jesus about His disciples, apparently hoping to interrogate them also.

Meanwhile, the high priest questioned Jesus about his disciples and his teaching.[55]

You see, if Peter had simply confessed that he was one of Christ's disciples, he would immediately have been taken indoors to stand right alongside his master.

Ever tried to get closer to God while still denying Him?

Peter did.

Peter's faith was limited because he thought its primary purpose was to help him see his own dreams realized. Being interrogated by the High Priest did not fit into that worldview.

So what kind of faith did Peter actually have?

Well, once while attending a dinner party, I was introduced to everyone by a member of my church congregation. The lady struggled to give me a title. She knew I was not officially a minister in her church but had seen me teach, preach, and lead. So in her desperation for an accurate description she announced I was a *quasi*-pastor.

The moment I got home, I looked up the word.

Quasi: almost but not quite, partly or pretending

For fun and in order to tease her in my next sermon, I announced my definition.

Quasi: nearly there, could do better, if only he had tried a little harder

Peter had what could be called *quasi*-faith. Nearly, but not quite the faith of Jesus. And as Peter followed Christ, his journey reads like a comical silent film where the hero constantly attempts new challenges only to fall down time and again.

He walks on water . . . only to sink.[56]

He humbles himself . . . only to be called Satan.[57]

He tries to hold onto three prophets . . . only to fall flat on his face.[58]

Each time, he dusts himself off and takes a step forward. Each time, he moves toward what he thinks is the final mountaintop. And each time, he is wrong.

Significantly, however, he is a little *less wrong* each time.

False summits make you realize that you never completely understood the challenge. You get to the top of your mountain only to realize it is still a long way from what God has in mind. Each summit, therefore, is a journey to bind us more and more to the kind of faith that Jesus had. Each time Peter is stretched, and each time he is given a greater faith.

But what is greater faith?

It is not *more* faith.

No, our lack of faith has little to do with its *size* and everything to do with its *shape*.

Quantum

In physics, quantum means:

> *The smallest quantity of energy; the smallest discrete quantity.*

The size of our faith is something that only we are obsessed with, not Jesus.

> *"I tell you the truth, if you had faith even as small as a mustard seed, you could say to this mountain, 'Move from here to there,' and it would move. Nothing would be impossible."*[59]

Jesus believes in *quantum* faith.

You see, success is not found in the *amount* of faith but in the *assimilation* of faith.

God wants us to have the same type of faith as Christ, a faith to believe for the same kind of outcome that Christ believes in. This is the point of the summit-shaped Kingdom Pattern. He takes us on the journey to discover His true purposes—a journey in which we will gain the kind of faith to believe for His dreams, rather than the kind of faith we need for our personal dreams.

Therefore, it is a path that time and again must highlight our *misunderstanding* of His purposes—a course where we succeed at what we thought was His ultimate idea only to find out that it wasn't.

After all, what is the point of having faith for the wrong plan?

Quasi-faith and quantum faith look different. Quantum faith steps out knowing it will hurt; quasi-faith only suspects it might.

In fact, quasi-faith seems to think that the whole point of faith is to believe that it won't hurt. The proponents of quasi-faith major on our *rights*. They tell us that if we have the faith to sacrifice, we have the right to be recompensed. However, Jesus, promoting quantum faith, majors on our *responsibilities*. If we have the faith to sacrifice, others may receive the Kingdom.

Peter's quasi-faith ran out when he realized his dream was about to hurt because it did not fit into what he thought the purpose of faith was. But things were changing. His faith was being replaced by a quantum of Jesus' faith. Like you and I tend to do, Peter lost footing for a while because he had a lot of faith for the wrong plan. Yet later, he became more effective with a small amount of faith for the right one.

What Christ did with Peter, He wishes to do with you and me. He took the little faith Peter had and showed him glimpses of success only to help him see how little they meant to Him. He then took him to a higher understanding of what real success looks like in the Kingdom of God.

Quasi-faith seeks *entitlement*, but quantum faith seeks *enlightenment*.

The story of Peter's denial provides only a glimpse into a life that walked the summits of faith. Each story moved Peter's faith closer to that of Jesus'. If you look closely, you can see it happen to him before your very eyes.

For Peter, the highs got higher and the lows were not quite as low as they used to be.

By the time of Peter's denial, his faith had already been growing. After all, he was one of only two disciples to follow Jesus into the temple court, the others had fled and not looked back. Ironically, his betrayal was due to the fact that he was beginning to understand that a violent victory was not what God had in mind. From my perspective at least, Peter's denial demonstrates that doubt in his own plan was beginning to set in. He was beginning to understand God's dream and in the transition from his quasi-faith to quantum faith, he fell into a spiritual valley that was actually higher than his previous mountaintops.

His faith was not simply getting *stronger* . . . It was getting *smarter*.

Discussion starters

Please take a look at these incidents from Peter's life. Then put the number for each one where you think he was on this Kingdom Pattern.

1. Peter accompanies Jesus into Jerusalem: John 12:12-13
2. Peter denies being Jesus' disciple: John 18:17
3. Peter walks on water: Matthew 14:29
4. Peter refuses to allow Jesus to wash his feet: John 13:8
5. Peter allows Jesus to wash his feet: John 13:9
6. Peter at the transfiguration of Jesus: Matthew 17:1-9
7. Peter speaks on the day of Pentecost: Acts 2:41

What is a key principle you see in Peter's summit-shaped journey?

Please share the principle on social media using: #kingdompatterns

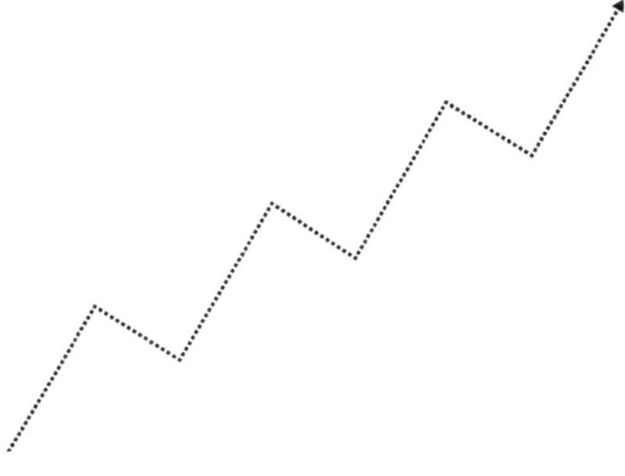

SUMMITS | The Practices

Leapfrog

Practice #1: *If you don't attempt the small peaks, you'll never get to the bigger ones!*

They are strategic. They are catalytic. They are prolific.

You cannot leapfrog God's plan. I mean, why would you want to? God has many phenomenal ideas in mind for you. Just look at what a simple fisherman from Galilee accomplished:

> He preached a sermon that led three thousand to join Jesus' mission.
>
> He wrote two epistles to the Church which became books of the Bible.
>
> He preached in Asia Minor for many years and founded the Church in Antioch.
>
> He later established a headquarters in Rome where he served as Bishop.
>
> He presided over the first Great Council in Jerusalem in 49 AD.
>
> He is now seen by some as the 'Prince of Apostles.'

Yet Peter's journey started with a simple, awkward, and unspectacular request.

Jesus got into his boat and asked him to:

> *"Put out into deep water, and let down the nets for a catch."*[60]

What if Peter had said no?[61]

Peter's bonding to Jesus' mission and the success he eventually experienced all started with a simple request:

> "Can I use your boat?"

I wonder, if Peter had ignored it and waited for a more grandiose challenge, would his pilgrimage have faltered at the very first hurdle? Could yours? Could there be lost-ness in your life because you ignored His simpler request? Could remembering and responding to it now lead you to greater faith?

Life's most important choices are the little ones.

Valley

Practice #2: *You have to first go down a mountain in order to climb up the next one!*

Take the short-term plunge. Find the middle ground. Gain a long-term view.

Getting to the next summit is not determined by whether or not you are prepared to climb up that mountain, but whether or not you are prepared to climb down the mountain you are presently on.

I have faced this challenge several times in my life. I was very happy at Sharon Church in Manchester. It was the church that I first attended when I became a Christian at age fourteen. I was baptized there. I was released into ministry there. I was believed in there. I was given space to pioneer and grow Pais, and was given a small salary to do it there.

One day, however, Pais grew too big for the facility.[62] Our training and conferences had outgrown the church property and our team was taking up too much space in the building. The DNA of Pais is one of bartering rather than buying; we do not like to spend money on bricks and mortar when we can trade our skills and expertise for space instead. So after some discussion, a nearby church of nineteen members offered us its huge worn building. The offer came with a condition: I must become the pastor of the church.

We were growing as an organization, and on the distant summit I could see a national headquarters, one large enough to house a training and resource center for our teams across the UK. I could also, however, see the valley I would need to descend into to make this happen. I would need to leave my home church and my salary to take over a church which could initially offer me no compensation. I would leave the support of many leaders and friends, as well as the security of an accountability system that had been working really well.

But, I had to go down before I could go up.

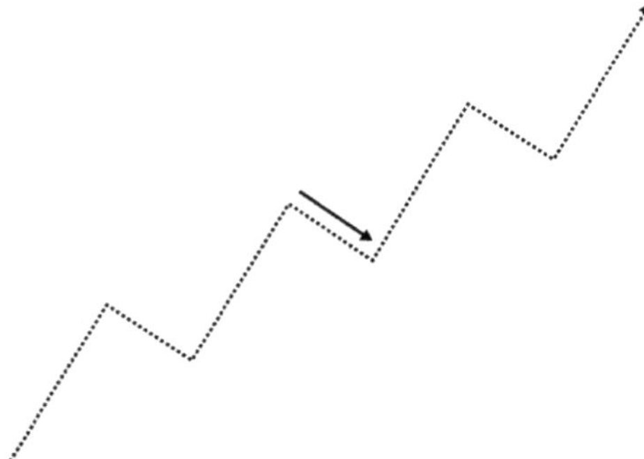

Similarly, five years later, I was asked to move to the United States. This Texas mega-church offered a good salary and the opportunity to create a global headquarters where I could connect with churches all over the States and build a worldwide influence. I could see a summit ahead, one where Pais would not just resource *a* nation but *many* nations.

However, I could also see a gigantic valley below.

I would have to start from scratch! I determined not take any of my great team with me because they were too vital to what we had been building in Manchester. I would also go from a full dance card of preaching opportunities in the UK to a blank slate where no one really knew me. Plus, I would lose the title 'Senior Pastor' to take up the position of an 'Associate Pastor.' In fact, although the original idea was for me to oversee the Pais apprentices, I volunteered to become the youth pastor.

I would go from a relatively big fish in a small pond to a small fish in a huge ocean.

> *One half of knowing what you want is knowing what you must give up before you get it.*[63]

A key part in the process of faith assimilation is the proactive decision to descend from one summit because you can see the potential of a higher summit in the distance.

You will therefore repeatedly be forced to lose your personal benefits for the sake of a greater impact. This repetition of the pattern gives you multiple choices and multiple chances to cut a new ravine in your hearts and minds. It is *tupos*, and it is helping you build your spiritual brawn and your supernatural toughness.

If you have ever been to a gym, you will know that lifting the weight is only part of the muscle building process. Lowering the weight builds muscle too.

I think this is perhaps the most faith-building exercise in God's gym.

Nestle

Practice #3: *Don't feather the nest!*

It is excessive. It is exclusive. It is exasperating.

When we reach a summit, we can be tempted to build a nest. We often want to get our friends around us and establish ourselves in such a way that we nestle into what is comfortable for us. After all, if our friends and family stop here, then it's okay for us, too . . . right?

That's what Peter thought when Moses and Elijah appeared at Jesus' transfiguration.

> *Peter said to Jesus, "Lord, it is good for us to be here. If you wish, I will put up three shelters—one for you, one for Moses, and one for Elijah."*[64]

Peter wanted to stay here because he wanted to be part of the gang. Who wouldn't? Imagine the things he would learn, the prestige he would gain. Just think of the benefits! This is a habit that many fall into, and by default it creates an exclusivity that becomes very difficult for others. Yet our desire to stay where we are can deny a spot into which others should move.

We see this in churches all the time. The Biblical example of leadership is that we pioneer, build, establish, and then put the young in charge while we go on to pioneer again. This is what I did in England when I moved to Texas. Modern Christianity has sometimes reversed that. We pioneer, establish ourselves, and then send the young out to pioneer for us.

Are you feathering your nest when instead you should be moving forward?

We are prone to do this as parents, mentors, business owners, and in any field of life when we think that faith is given so we can stay comfortable. Instead, for the sake of advancing God's dream, we sometimes have to move off a mountain so someone else can move up it. This should not be automatically interpreted as a prompt to leave a position you hold, but rather to ask whether or not you can reach new heights and by doing so create space for others to flourish.

Inevitably, those of us who make a nest knock others off our perch. Our temptation to hold onto our summit creates an insecurity that not only limits us, but limits them. How many of our children, employees, and disciples had their faith stifled because *we* refused to move on?

When we roost, we rot.

Failure

Practice #4: *Acknowledge that failure is also summit-shaped!*

Face reality. Understand reality. Change reality.

The problem with failure is that it contains the occasional success.

For the sake of an analogy that most readers will understand, let's take for example what this could look like in a church. In this hypothetical congregation, God is speaking to the leadership about why the numbers are decreasing and, more importantly, why its influence in the community is also diminishing. The leadership is forced to ask themselves hard questions, and doubts begin to set in, which in this case is a good thing! Questions arise concerning their present methodology, which does not seem to be fulfilling the vision that God has placed within them. Yet, just when the doubts are beginning to do their job and possible changes are about to be implemented, the worst possible thing happens:

A couple of new families join the church. A large financial donation is received. The musicians excel and the worship goes to another level for a few months.

Please forgive the hyperbole of people joining a church as 'the worst possible thing,' but in my heart of hearts I sadly believe that our *reaction* to such events is detrimental to God's plans.

You see, failure is also a slow process of zig zags.

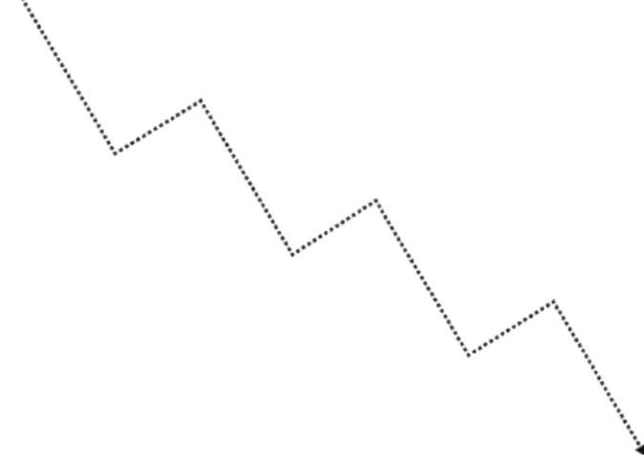

The highs are not as high as they used to be and the lows keep getting lower. Yet because of these occasional successes, there is a sigh of relief and the fresh challenge of the Holy Spirit is once again put on the back burner. For some reading this book, facing the reality of failure might be the first step required of you to see eventual success.

Yet, be encouraged—if you notice a shadow, there must be a mountain nearby!

Tourism

Practice #5: *Keep moving forward!*

Don't just look up. Don't forget to look back. Don't let looks deceive you.

As you keep moving forward, you will naturally move upward.

Remember, the pilgrimage is not to get to a particular mountain; it is to grow in the same type of faith that Jesus had and for the same purpose that He had it. We climb not to gain a title, a trophy, or a trinket, but a token of faith—the type of faith that moves mountains. As we stretch ourselves and move forward, each summit deposits a greater perspective of God's vision within us.

We do not settle. We are tourists. . . . As was Peter. He kept moving forward, never staying at one stage of faith. Always looking to the next summit, he constantly increased his ability to impact the world even when things seemed bleak.

According to tradition, he died at the hands of Nero, persecuted and crucified upside down. Of Peter's final days, we are told that he was cast into a terrible Roman prison called the Mamertine and for nine months, in absolute darkness, he endured monstrous torture manacled to a post. Yet also according to tradition, in spite of all the suffering Peter was subjected to, he converted his jailers, Processus, Martinianus, and forty-seven others.[65]

The blood of the martyrs is the seed of the church. — Tertullian

At the end of his life, Peter's new low was still much higher than when he walked into Jerusalem by the side of Jesus, confident in a plan he had little idea was wrong. His life was a series of highs that got higher and lows that were higher in the advancement of the Kingdom of God than many of his previous successes. Without knowing exactly where he would end up, he moved forward, never settling on a mountain or giving up in a valley.

His life is a great lesson to us all because, when you climb up a physical mountain, it feels like you are getting nowhere. The view as you look up seems constant. In fact, it can be a little soul destroying—that is until you look behind you and notice that the scenery has changed far more quickly than you expected.

It is the same spiritually. When climbing a summit, you may not feel you are making much progress, but when you look back, you will be shocked at how far you have actually come.

Discussion starters

Practice #1: *If you don't attempt the small peaks, you'll never reach the bigger ones!*

Practice #2: *You have to first go down a mountain in order to climb up the next one!*

Practice #3: *Don't feather the nest!*

Practice #4: *Acknowledge that failure is also summit-shaped!*

Practice #5: *Keep moving forward!*

1. Which of these practices seems most relevant to you at this point in your journey?
2. What is the next practical step for you to take?
3. What questions do you still have?
4. What advice that I have not written would you give someone journeying on this pattern?
5. Please share your advice and questions on social media using: #kingdompatterns

KINGDOM PATTERN

SPHERES

SPHERES | The Pattern

Peace

Calling is sphere-shaped.

When Jesus was around thirty years old, His mission was affirmed:

> *When all the people were being baptized, Jesus was baptized too. And as he was praying, heaven was opened and the Holy Spirit descended on him in bodily form like a dove. And a voice came from heaven: "You are my Son, whom I love; with you I am well pleased."*[66]

The Holy Spirit *descended* like a dove, but He is *not* a dove.

He is not a pigeon or a parrot either.

The problem with referring to the Holy Spirit as a dove, or indicating His characteristics are similar, is that it can lead us to think He is in some ways skittish and easily frightened away. This is particularly harmful to a Kingdom Pattern through which God uses people to 'build-out' our calling. Pastor and teacher, Donald Gee, once said:

> *There are times when disunity is a sign of life and unity a sign of death.*

Many Christians struggle with that quote because one of the more destructive influences on the path to finding God's direction has become the esteem, elevation, and exaltation of '*peace*.'

It has given rise to questions such as, "Do you have a peace about it?" And comments like, "God won't lead you down a path where there is confusion and conflict."

Sure, God is not a God of confusion, but that does not mean that you will not occasionally be confused by what He does. In fact, if Christians always felt peaceful, I am sure non-believers would excuse our faithfulness in the same way that Satan undermined Job's. Approaching the Creator, the devil (meaning accuser) suggested that Job was only worshipping Him because he had lived a blessed life.

> *"Does Job fear God for nothing?" Satan replied.*[67]

In other words, he intimated that Job only served God because God served Job!

You see, although our faith may be tested on our summits, it is studied by others in our valleys. It is when we turn to face life struggles that our lives can most effectively point others to the hope we have in God.

> *Some might say they don't believe in heaven. Go and tell it to the man who lives in hell.*[68]

Therefore we must not avoid the reality God wants us to grow through nor spiritualize our excuses to run from it.

Especially in the one area that is key to understanding our full calling:

Relationship.

A few years ago I was trying to help a couple of colleagues deal with the disappointments that one had with the leadership style of the other. We walked into a very small office that just about fit the three of us, and the leader brought out a guitar. He desperately wanted to start with worship because, in my opinion, he desperately wanted to delay the conversation. I stopped the impromptu singing session

as I could see his team member was simply just too frustrated and first needed to talk. I was, of course, blamed by the leader for stifling the Holy Spirit.

We must understand that there is a distinct difference between being at rest with God about a decision and no longer feeling a battle in our emotions. Life will often become more 'peaceful' when we fail to pursue a godly course of action and disengage with difficult people. In fact, if we push the self-escape button, we will often immediately feel *'peace'* . . . but we are likely to suffer the consequences after an initial respite. I have seen many people opt out of a commitment and, in doing so, self-eject into a spiritual wilderness where they wander and wonder why they seem so unable to find God's path. They misinterpreted the instant relief that comes to all humans when we relinquish a responsibility with the supernatural peace that comes from the divine.

And it's a problem.

Why?

Because misdirection comes when we seek peace above purpose.

And missteps are common when we seek purpose without people.

In this Kingdom Pattern, you will find that your relationships are key to both finding and fulfilling your calling, as well as spotting where you are in that process.

Bat-Kol

It's interesting that the confirmation of Jesus' mission came in the form of *'Bat-Kol.'*

> *And a voice came from heaven: "You are my Son . . ."* [69]

Bat-Kol is the Hebrew phrase for a direct voice from God with no visible medium such as a prophet or priest. It literally means *'daughter of a voice*' and, interestingly, Jewish tradition says that God especially communicated this way *after* the death of the prophets.

> *After the death of Haggai, Zechariah and Malachi, the last of the prophets, the Holy Spirit ceased from Israel; nevertheless they received communications from God through the medium of Bat-Kol.*[70]

Christian scholars also refer to a direct voice from Heaven in a similar way, interpreting the words to mean an '*echo*' voice. Significantly, both 'daughter of' and 'echo' infer that God sees *Bat-Kol* as secondary and *inferior* to prophecy!

In other words, and here is the kicker: *Bat-Kol* is God's last resort!

When God has no prophets available or when we are so unspiritual that we will not listen to them, He speaks to us via *Bat-Kol*. In fact, He will rarely use an audible voice with someone who is spiritually mature or on the right track.[71]

Which is odd because we definitely don't see it that way, do we?

I'm sure that many of us would much prefer it if God gave us direction directly from Heaven, audibly and as clear as a bell. In fact, I am fairly certain that we would idolize those who said that they received their vision or guidance this way.

So why would God prefer things differently?

A key may be found in the Jewish Encyclopedia which happens to mention that:

> *The Holy Spirit rested upon the Prophets, and the intercourse was personal and intimate; while those that heard the Bat-Ḳol stood in no relation whatever to the Holy Spirit.*

Bat-Kol requires no relationship.

It requires no relationship with God and no relationship with His body, the Church.

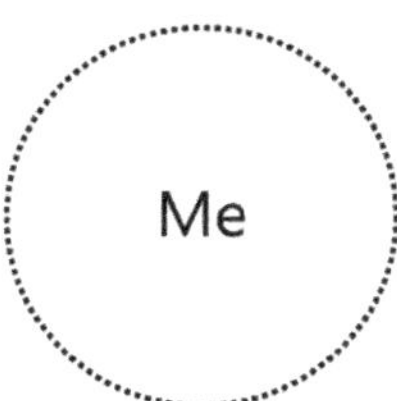

No relationship is simpler. No relationship is easier. No relationship has a border that cannot be crossed and a barrier that cannot be broken through. But no relationship is less effective when it comes to God's purpose of binding us to His calling by binding us to one another.

> *Now I rejoice in what I am suffering for you, and I fill up in my flesh what is still lacking in regard to Christ's afflictions, for the sake of his body, which is the church.*[72]

At Jesus' baptism, God spoke dramatically, but nothing really changed. No one was transformed.

Not even Jesus.

Influence

When God wants to build out my calling, He prefers to do it through other people's spheres of influence, either indirectly via the Bible or directly via relationships. The Holy Spirit uses His Word and His people to teach, challenge, rebuke, inform, and inspire me.

He is not so much the vehicle but the catalyst.

This was His plan from the very beginning even before I was in my mother's womb. Remarkably, before the fall, when Adam had a perfect character and when His relationship with the Father was as pure as the driven snow, God made a shocking observation:

> *"It is not good for the man to be alone."*[73]

What?

Alone! He was with God and everything was perfect, and therefore surely everything was good! Yes, it was, but as the saying goes, the *good* is often the enemy of the *great*. God's plans for you are not just good—they are great!

So when we seek *independent* rather than *interdependent* direction, we choose to ignore the Kingdom Pattern He has chosen to develop our effectiveness, and so we begin the slide into lost-ness.

This particular pilgrimage is perhaps best explained in the letter to the Ephesians:

> *It was he who gave some to be apostles, some to be prophets, some to be evangelists, and some to be pastors and teachers, to prepare God's people for works of service, so that the body of Christ may be built up until we all reach unity in the faith and in the knowledge of the Son of God and become mature . . .* [74]

God will prepare you for His service through His people. Using the example of these five gifts, we can see why this Kingdom Pattern is at work in our lives. Although it is in no way limited to these gifts, they provide a simple way to unpack it.[75]

The Kingdom Pattern of the spheres is intended to develop your vision by uncovering talents, gifts, and the elements of your calling that would otherwise be hidden. In this way, God will repeatedly send people into your life to shape you. Essentially, this repeated pattern will pull out dormant elements of God's calling in your life. However, *if* they are allowed to shape you, *how* and to what *extent*

they shape you will depend on your ability to understand the dynamic of this Kingdom Pattern.

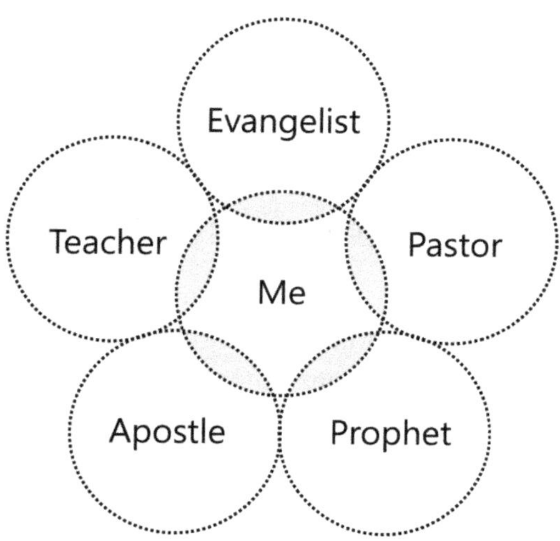

One of the first people who influenced my calling was an evangelist. Paul Morley took me on the streets of Manchester City Centre shopping district and helped me understand how to attract a crowd and not repel them—how to connect with a group of strangers rather than appear strange to a group of consumers. He taught me how to publicly share my story. He gave me opportunities that brought out an unrealized creativity to communicate my faith to those unfamiliar with it.

Harry Letson was a pastor. My pastor. He taught me the dynamics of providing pastoral support. He showed me how to help those with difficult issues in their lives, how to deal with conflicts, and how to heal. He helped me uncover a sensitivity towards people and the dormant ability I had to help them find God in their circumstances.

Both Paul and Harry helped shape my calling.

They also helped me realize something else:

I am *not* an evangelist or a pastor!

The key to a successful journey through this Kingdom Pattern is the ability to decipher what parts of other people's spheres God wants you to absorb and what parts He does not.

In other words, when He exposes you to others and their lives overlap yours, there is something about them that He wants to become *part of* you.

But He does not want you to become *them*!

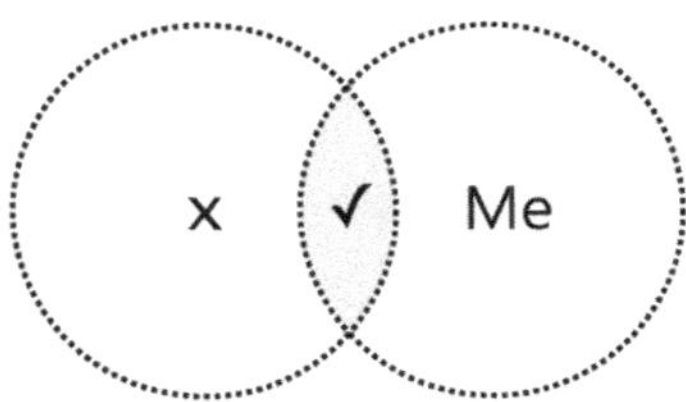

This Kingdom Pattern acts like a vending machine. It provides whatever I am willing to pay for.

Because we have to pay for relationships, right?

Those we love the most hurt us the most, and those we learn from the most will likely challenge us the most.

Yet this exchanging of our spheres means we must lose something of ourselves in order to gain something of ourselves.

If we are not willing to pay that price, if we are not willing to discover God's calling in our lives through the lives of others, then the following promise will not be fulfilled:

> *. . . attaining to the whole measure of the fullness of Christ . . .* [76]

Let me remind you of the reason for walking these patterns . . .

> *... Then we will no longer be infants, tossed back and forth by the waves, and blown here and there by every wind of teaching and by the cunning and craftiness of people in their deceitful scheming.*[77]

I cannot list the number of great men and women who have become part of my pilgrimage. What I can say, however, is this: if I had not correctly absorbed their influence, my vision would not be on the way to becoming fully whole.

My calling would be dented.

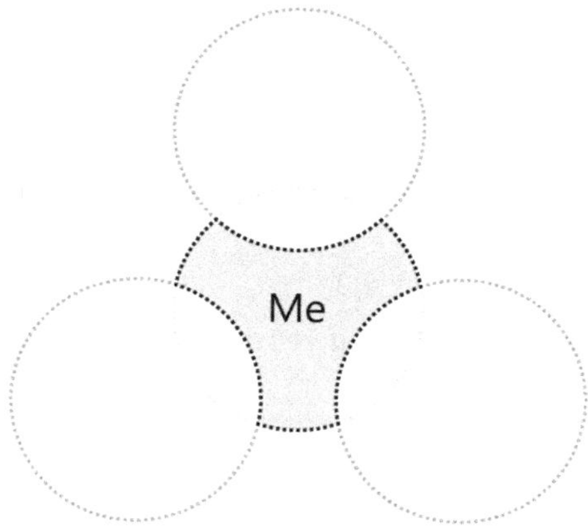

Finding God's direction will be far easier when you can spot whom He is bringing into your life and why He is bringing them your way. You see, understanding the calling God has on your life requires a high degree of maturity.

Immaturity declares, "I am not easily influenced," and that proud naivety makes us vulnerable to the schemes of the devil and people.

Maturity, however, recognizes that we are all easily influenced and that wisdom is found in allowing the right influences into our lives in the right amounts. It is not found in full separation nor full integration, but in astute spherical calculations.

Therefore, walking this Kingdom Pattern requires what I believe is key to relational maturity:

> Putting ourselves in the path of others in order to influence *and* be influenced by them.

Now, who do we know that was good at doing that?

Discussion starters

1. Please write in three influences in your life depicted by the three circles.
2. Which parts of your calling is God building out in you through those influences?
3. Are there other influences you need to allow into your sphere? If so, list them below.
4. Is there an additional principle you see in the pattern that is not stated in the book?
5. Please share your thoughts on social media using: #kingdompatterns

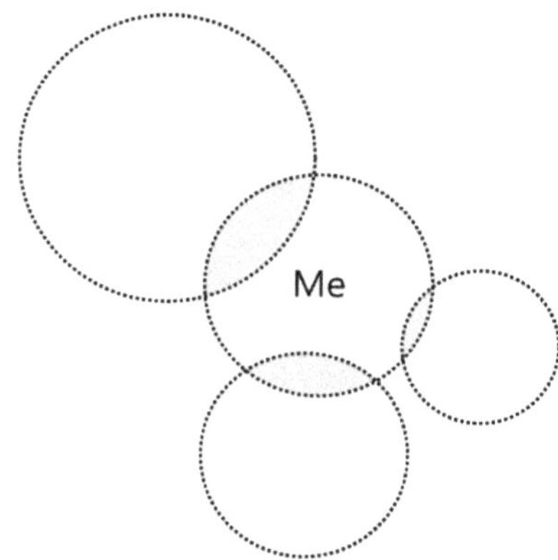

Y

SPHERES | The Pilgrim

Superhero

Jesus was fully human, not superhuman.

> *Now Jesus himself was about thirty years old when he began his ministry. He was the son, so it was thought, of Joseph . . .* [78]

Unlike a modern comic book superhero, Jesus did not receive His power by being bitten by a radioactive bug in some science lab experiment gone wrong. It was passed onto Him as result of His relationship with His Father. How He *fulfilled* His calling, however, was shaped by those whose spheres of influence He allowed to overlap with His.

Jesus was a man placed in time. He had a history, a culture, and a circle of relationships that were not irrelevant to who He was, but vital to His calling. Significantly, the *Bat-Kol* at Christ's baptism was followed in the scripture by a varied list of people in His genealogy. One of them was His cousin John. And it was John who was responsible for the breaking through of the Kingdom, not Jesus.

> *And from the time John the Baptist began preaching until now, the Kingdom of Heaven has been forcefully advancing, and violent people are attacking it.*[79]

It was not until *after* John's imprisonment that Jesus was fully released into His ministry.

When Jesus heard that John had been put in prison, he withdrew to Galilee . . . From that time on Jesus began to preach, "Repent, for the kingdom of heaven has come near."[80]

A few scholars believe that this was because Jesus was a disciple of John. As disputed as that idea may be,[81] only when John had come to the end of his ministry did Jesus take up His cousin's baton and run with it. The reason for this may be partly found in what I once considered to be the most shocking statement in the Bible:

Jesus learned *obedience.*[82]

This does not mean that He was once disobedient, but part of its meaning is that, to fulfill His calling *completely,* Christ would acquire the experience and know-how of others.

Are you surprised by this? I was. Yet the evidence, as you will see, is overwhelming.

Pharisees

Let me share just four of the groups who influenced the most influential figure in history.

Perhaps the most surprising of these might be the Pharisees.

This influential sect helped shape His *training* of others.

Many messianic scholars see Jesus not as one *outside* the Pharisaical sect, but as one who, while not an actual Pharisee, was an *insider* to their wider movement and therefore embarrassed by their actions. Note, for instance, that the Pharisees would rarely socialize with anyone outside their party. Yet they often had Jesus around for dinner.

When giving direction to His own disciples, Jesus uses the Pharisees as both a negative and a positive example. This is partly due to the fact that they were generally on the same page as He was. Unlike the Sadducees, the Pharisees also sought a new Kingdom. In fact,

Jesus had so much in common with the Pharisees[83] and vice versa that some of them tried to come to His rescue, warning Him about Herod's plot against Him.[84]

Listen carefully to what Jesus commands His closest followers:

> *The teachers of the law and the Pharisees sit in Moses' seat. So you must obey them and do everything they tell you. But do not do what they do, for they do not practice what they preach.*[85]

Jesus' commandment to His disciples shows that He understood the key principle of this Kingdom Pattern: incorporate what you should and leave the rest. Sadly, we often choose to reject the influence of those God places in our lives, using their flaws as an excuse.

Jesus did not.

Sages

A second group whose sphere influenced Jesus were the sages.

These prominent men helped shape His *teaching* style.

Hillel was around thirty years older than Christ, and elements of his seven rules of exegesis were used regularly by the Son of God.[86] Perhaps the most famous is the Messiah's practice of *kal v'chomer* or 'light and heavy.' This was a method that Hillel taught, encouraging his followers in the use of specific metaphoric comparisons.

Listen to how Jesus' teaching employs the sages' method:

> *Or if he asks for a fish, will give him a snake? If you, then, though you are evil, know how to give good gifts to your children, how much more will your Father in heaven give good gifts to those who ask him!*[87]

This statement would get an A+ from Hillel.

Many of Jesus' parables, such as those involving a 'king' figure, were twists on similar pre-existing stories. The parable of the sower is His take on the 'Parable of the Four Hearers,' a common parable in Jewish teaching. Various twists on it can be found, such as Gamaliel's parable of four fish or the parable of the four kitchen utensils, each of them highlighting the four ways a person hears and responds to truth.[88] The parable of the sower, therefore, follows a clear tradition in storytelling that Jesus *learned* from others, committed to, and executed very well.

Neither the Sermon on the Mount nor the Lord's Prayer were completely original. For instance, all elements of the message on the mountain can be found in previous Jewish writings[89] and the most famous of all prayers is actually Christ's summary of the Jewish 'Amidah.'[90]

Jesus' unique quality is this: He helped reveal the truth by cutting and pasting previous teaching, chipping away men's traditions, and introducing new facets that emphasized what was closest to God's intention.

When referring to the use of the sages' teaching by Jesus, Pinchas Lapide explains:

> Beethoven did not invent a single new note to compose the Ninth Symphony . . .[91]

The composer took notes that already existed but then put them together in such a way that the world discovered the music we had never heard in them before. The notes were always there and so in some way the tune had always existed, but it took Beethoven to reveal it to us.

Jesus did the same—not with music, but with truth.

Hasidim

Thirdly, the original Hasidim were the fore-runners of the Pharisees.

This sect shaped the charismatic *style* of Jesus' ministry.

Living in and around the north shore of Galilee, these mystics were famous for fantastic results in prayer. They would not allow anything to distract them when engaging in their efforts, and so they commanded that when their disciples were on mission: "*Even if the King greets a man, he must not return the greeting.*"[92]

Similarly, Jesus reminds His disciples:

> "*Do not take a purse or bag or sandals; and do not greet anyone on the road.*"[93]

The Hasidim practiced a certain form of meditation before they prayed, which Jesus adopted when He interceded for Jairus's daughter.[94] In doing so, He expelled people from the room and only took Peter in with Him. Peter is seen to then carry on the practice when he raised Dorcas from the dead.[95] The *way* that Jesus healed, including the purposeful use of dramatic gestures, was guided by the example of the Hasidim and, according to the expert Shmuel Safrai, Jesus had more in common with this group than any other in that era of history.

Essenes

Fourthly, the Essenes not only influenced Jesus, but also His forerunner John.

They impacted the *politics* of Jesus.

By politics, I simply mean the way in which we organize ourselves in a community. Some have suggested that John the Baptist was once a member of the Essenes, but there is only circumstantial evidence

for this. Without doubt, however, the Essenes' ideas on community are seen in the commands of John and Jesus.

I am, of course, not saying that they taught Jesus His beliefs, but the way in which they understood community gave Jesus examples of what a godly community on earth might look like. For instance, their sharing of possessions when joining the family of believers was a key facet of the Essenes' vision.

> *"And if someone wants to sue you and take your shirt, let him have your coat as well."*[96]

Jesus emphasized that it was a community, not simply a theology, which would prepare the way of the Lord. However, Jesus moved away from the Essenes on how this point was played out. The sect showed a strong desire for exclusivity. They rejected the temple system and left Jerusalem in 200 BC when a high priest was appointed who was not acceptable to them.

Jesus used some of their practices, but rejected their pride.

As with the other three groups already mentioned, He was unrecognizable to the Essenes as the Messiah because He did not fit their image of what the Anointed One would look like. Yet He recognized in them ideas and concepts that could make His ministry impactful and His explanations more holistic.

Jesus may be an odd choice for this particular Kingdom Pattern. Yet more than any of the apostles or any other Biblical character . . .

He is its shining example.

Courage

I wonder sometimes why a pattern so clear in the Bible is so uncomfortable to understand.

Currently in the United States, political polarization has led to what is being labelled the 'culture wars.' We seem to have lost the ability to see the good in those we disagree with and the bad in those 'on our side.' Recent experiments have shown that social media has acted as a catalyst for this.[97] It is as though, unlike the pilgrim Jesus, we cannot pick the meat from the bones. Maybe it is because we feel that if we agree with someone in one aspect, then we are by default agreeing with them in every aspect. Or maybe it is worse than that.

Maybe it is simply cowardice.

I was once privileged to spend a couple of days with an author whose reputation was controversial. I wanted to ask Brian about a book I was working on because after reading one of his earliest works,[98] I thought he might have insights on some of my historical references.

During our final conversation, I asked Brian what I planned to be my last question: "What advice would you give me as I lead Pais?"

He initially replied, "Be prepared for your audience to shrink when they realize your beliefs on more contentious subjects." At that point I suddenly realized that my friend had presumed I had read some of his more controversial books . . . but I had not. So I told Brian that he would probably consider my theology fairly orthodox, but that I would be happy for him to challenge me on those more disputed topics in our last conversation.

What he said next blew me away.

> "No."

He then went on to explain:

> "Paul, what you are doing is a great work for the Kingdom. If God is not leading you to ask those questions, then I do not want to distract you from the clear calling He has given you."

I cannot tell you how impressed I was with that!

The key to this Kingdom Pattern is knowing what to take on board to build out your calling and what to avoid that may cripple it. Jesus understood that. Yet unlike His example, some of us are afraid to be associated with those whose views differ from ours. Maybe we feel that we can be justified because of Paul's words:

> *But now I am writing to you that you must not associate with anyone who claims to be a brother or sister but is sexually immoral or greedy, an idolater or slanderer, a drunkard or swindler. Do not even eat with such people.*[99]

However, I don't believe we can use this passage to camouflage our motives and fear. I think Paul's rebuke of Peter may more accurately describe this darker side of our actions:

> *When Cephas [Peter] came to Antioch, I opposed him to his face, because he stood condemned. For before certain men came from James, he used to eat with the Gentiles. But when they arrived, he began to draw back and separate himself from the Gentiles because he was afraid of those who belonged to the circumcision group.*[100]

I have a far more orthodox view on the afterlife, sexual orientation, and other doctrines than Brian, but if I allow my cowardice and other people's opinion to rob me of what God can teach me through him, will I struggle to fully realize the potential within me?

After all, how did Jesus' sphere influence so many different people?

Because He allowed so many different people to influence Him.

Discussion starters

Based on my descriptions of the groups who influenced Jesus, draw spheres intersecting with the circle above to show how much influence He allowed from them. Label each accordingly.

1. Pharisees
2. Essenes
3. Sages
4. Hasidim

What is a key principle you see in Jesus' sphere-shaped journey?

Please share the principle on social media using: #kingdompatterns

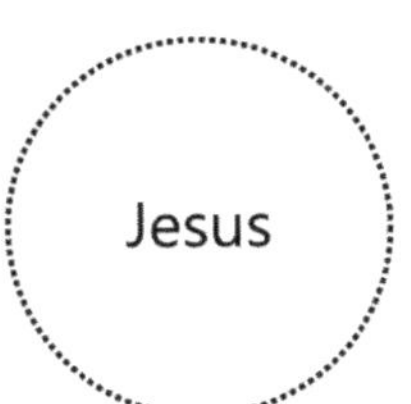

SPHERES | The Practices

Dummy

Practice #1: *Learn to discern!*

Is it imagination? Is it manipulation? Is it revelation?

How do you know if the guidance you are being given by people is from God?

Earlier in the book I stated that patterns trump prophecies, but hopefully you understood that I still believe very much in the power of the supernatural. So when someone speaks into your life saying that God has told them to tell you something, how do you know if it is divine or not?

When someone speaks on behalf of God, it is either *imagination, manipulation,* or *revelation.*

Let me share with you a couple of simple thoughts that may help you with this. Please note that this is not meant to be a comprehensive 'fool's guide' to discerning the voice of God. These thoughts are simply basic principles that I have found helpful.

If it is *imagination,* it may not be particularly harmful, but it may distract you from God's real intention. The usual sign is that it is ambiguous and cannot be put to the test. If it is God, you can usually see something within it that only God would have known or know to do.

If it is *manipulation,* it may indeed be harmful to you. A clue might be that its message is separated from things God has previously said to you. Remember, God uses repetition. Even when He speaks in a new format and uses new people, there will be something familiar about His message that connects to something you know for sure He has previously said.

If it is *revelation*, it will be harmful to the devil. The indication will be that it will reveal something that advances the Kingdom in an even greater way than you were able to accomplish before. It will be in line with the Bible, in line with the character of God, and will reveal an answer to our question: "What can I do that will most advance the Kingdom of God?"

Bearing these thoughts in mind will help us avoid another divisive scheme of our day: the using of the Holy Spirit as a ventriloquist dummy.

Intentionally or unintentionally, we can make God say things we want Him to say. For instance, a common problem in the Church is that some of us make commitments, only to opt out of them before fulfilling our promises. Sometimes, in order to validate our unfaithfulness, we argue that God's Spirit has led us into our decision. We must learn to discern when God's Spirit is leading us into something and also when our flesh is leading us out of it.

The latter may provide light relief, but it almost always leads to lost-ness.

A simple litmus test:

The Holy Spirit will never lead you to break His Word . . . or your word.

Roots

Practice #2: *Learn to spread your roots wide!*

It will attract more people. It will attract the right people. It will make you more attractive.

A long time ago, a Christian leader approached me with what he called 'a word from God.'

> *Paul, I think God sees you like a tree whose roots, rather than going very deep, have stretched very wide. You have and you will continue to find new sources of nutrition and feed in places outside of those in your network. This will lead to a tree with wide branches that numerous and many types of birds will be able to find shelter in.*

It was part observation and part prediction.

In both parts he was correct. I've worked hard over the years to pull wisdom, knowledge, and experience from many different places. I have seen the dangers of only drawing from one source of thinking. Doing so can limit *who* you can work with, *how* you can work with them, and *what* can be achieved.

Pais is a non-denominational organization with secular partnerships. If I only read the books my friends read and only listened to the teaching my denomination taught, I would never have been able to gather the people we needed for this global work. Currently we have many ethnicities on Pais working on six continents. Spreading my roots has allowed other Christian traditions to make our efforts more holistic . . . and healthier. Going deep into only one source rather than spreading our roots would not stretch our thinking and, importantly, not uncover those God-given revelations that lie dormant within us.

To find God's direction, you need to expose yourself to it.

Spatial

Practice #3: *Choose influences wisely!*

Ask, "Are they too far away?" Ask, "Are they too close?" Ask, "Am I creating the right space?"

It is generally true to say that relationships are both *special* and *spatial* and that there are no bad relationships, just *spatial miscalculations.*[101]

Handled correctly, any relationship can help you uncover something of God latent within you. However, we can often have the wrong people too close to us and the right people too far away.

> *So they signaled their partners in the other boat to come and help them, and they came and filled both boats so full that they began to sink.*[102]

Have you noticed that when Jesus first called some of His disciples, their response often required more than simply reaching out to Him? Once hearing His voice, they usually had to reach out for others. Often a Biblical hero who met God in a desert, a trance, a dream, or some other life-changing experience *immediately* had to find someone to help them take hold of what they had just been told to do.

This process will be true of your calling also.

However, simply connecting with others will not make His dream come true. You have to work out how to give your life away appropriately. Christ, for instance, did not run around trying to give the same amount of time to everyone. He had a different level of investment in His disciples to that of the crowds. Even within His circle of disciples, Jesus had a closer connection with some than others.

So if we are to be fully rounded people, able to fully grasp the mission God has given us, we should not look for a single mentor, but instead look for *mentors*. I would advise that you find people with a track record of success in the specific areas you are looking for

guidance in. Then find other influencers for other areas of your life. No one is an expert in everything! For instance, there are those I would ask for theological advice that I might not ask to help me become a better communicator. There are great communicators that I may not approach to teach me how to become a better father.

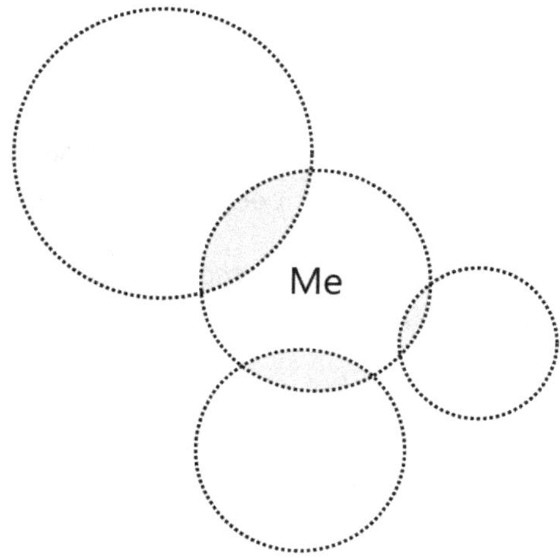

Yet so often we limit ourselves to so few people.

Why?

The sad truth is that we allow people's personalities to influence our decisions more than the fruit of their lives. Those we dislike we keep at a distance, and those we find easy to connect with we allow to interfere too much—even when they are clearly not qualified to do so.

Can I encourage you to be bold enough to ask for help from those whose lives prove they have insight into what you need and have the courage to not rely on the same people for everything?

Sometimes we don't *miss* God's direction in our lives . . .

We *mis*manage it.

Teresa

Practice #4: *Learn to enlarge the circle around you!*

Love God. Love yourself. Love others.

Don't filter God by filtering people.

> *The biggest problem in the world today is that we draw the circle around us too small.* — Mother Teresa[103]

It was Mother Teresa's understanding of this Kingdom Pattern that allows her legacy and story to cross religious boundaries. She was a woman of compassion and her sphere of influence reaches into the lives of those who are not of her Roman Catholic faith.

Jesus also challenged us to draw a circle bigger than the one drawn by those not of the Kingdom.

> *If you love those who love you, what reward will you get? Are not even the tax collectors doing that?*[104]
>
> *If all you do is love the lovable, do you expect a bonus? Anybody can do that.*[105]
>
> *If you are kind only to your friends, how are you different from anyone else? Even pagans do that.*[106]

It is this last translation that connects our Kingdom Pattern so closely with the purpose of the three *Kingdom Trilogy* books. We must not be like the pagans who asked God to bless their chosen relationship, but instead we must seek first the Kingdom by asking God for the relationships to which He directs us.

I once asked an experienced leader how I could grow Pais, and he suggested that I spend some time with a different type of Christian leader than my Pentecostal friends. For instance, he said, "Why not spend a couple of weeks in a monastery!" Bizarrely, however, before I had time to put it into action, I was led to leave the UK and work with a Texas mega-church . . . not exactly what I think he had in mind. To be honest, it could have been intimidating, but if I have learned anything on my journey it is this:

> Insecurity will limit your vision.

Remember, God did not bring a person into your life because He prefers them to *you*. He created *you* because *you* were who He wanted *you* to be. That is why He made sure you won the first race you ever entered. Think about it. At a very young age, you entered your mother's womb with thousands of other contenders . . . and took first prize.

You are who He wants!

It is just that He sees a bigger you in you than you do!

Discussion starters

Practice #1: *Learn to discern!*
Practice #2: *Learn to spread your roots wide!*
Practice #3: *Choose influences wisely!*
Practice #4: *Learn to enlarge the circle around you!*

1. Which of these practices seems most relevant to you at this point in your journey?
2. What is the next practical step for you to take?
3. What questions do you still have?
4. What advice that I have not written would you give someone journeying on this pattern?
5. Please share your advice and questions on social media using: #kingdompatterns

KINGDOM PATTERN

RINGS

RINGS | The Pattern

Radar

Momentum is ring-shaped.

Have you ever felt that your life is going around in circles? Well, perhaps it is.

Although we eagerly desire to see our lives make headway, we sometimes feel stuck in the same routines that deliver the same results. It is a problem. After all, how can we become a catalyst for the advancement of the Kingdom of God if we ourselves cannot take the next step forward?

A typical reoccurring scene in old black and white war movies involves a radar on a submarine. A crew member will spot an approaching vessel and point to the beep on the radar which appears every time a sweep is completed.

Beep. Beep. Beep.

God's direction in our lives can often resemble a beep on a radar.

I am sure you have experienced this. During certain seasons, you start to hear the same message wherever you go. You might be on vacation and visit a new church where the minister preaches the same sermon you just heard at home. Friends, family, relatives, even people who don't know you pray the same thing over you. Or maybe a distinctive theme, subject, or lesson constantly jumps off the page of the Bible no matter what passage you seem to be reading.

Beep. Beep. Beep.

Each beep is a warning signal, not necessarily of impending doom but of impending opportunity. Each points out a link, preparing us to make the transition into the next season of our lives. These connections usually last longer than an instance but have limited availability.

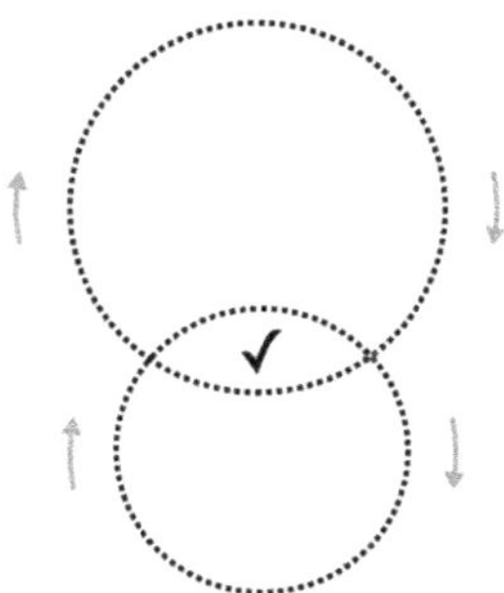

Solomon, described as one of the wisest men in history, said:

> *The way of the wise winds upwards!*[107]

It is true. To create momentum, we have to wind things up—like a clockwork toy whose spring we turn until it can turn no more—and then let it go.

In fact, you've probably heard the expression 'wind up' used for repeatedly teasing someone time after time in order to finally get a reaction. In the UK, those who provoke people in this way are known as 'wind-up merchants.' Another use of the phrase is to say that someone will 'wind up' in trouble. Again, this communicates the idea that after a repetition of a certain type of behavior there will be an eventual and inevitable climactic result.

God does not plan for you to wind up in trouble, but in a new season of life. However, it will not just 'happen'; there will be something *new* you need to do, say, or think to make the connection. There will be a moment when you need to *act*.

Miss it and you may miss out . . . at least for the foreseeable future.

Scripture records Jabez smartly praying:

> *"Oh, that you would bless me and enlarge my territory!"*[108]

It was a good prayer because God's desire is to constantly enlarge our capacity for the purpose of advancing His Kingdom.

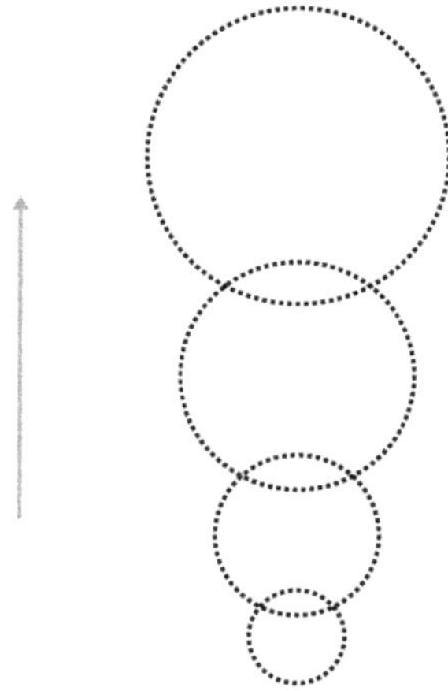

Many years ago, however, I remember a popular book that led some to believe that if they simply repeated the prayer regularly, it would just happen. It won't.

To move upwards from one ring to another, we need to spot the opportunity God is providing and make the necessary adjustments. This may require a new level of maturity and will certainly bring new challenges. The trouble is that getting older does not guarantee that we become more spiritually astute. In fact, as we grow older, we sometimes find it harder to change. So this Kingdom Pattern is repeated to help us connect, not just once, but many times throughout our lives. This *tupos* is designed to make new actions and upward transition natural to us.

Put simply, the more often we change, the easier change becomes.

Binah

Ironically, the purpose of repetition is momentum.

Solomon understood that our lives will either wind upwards or wind downwards, leading to atrophy. The key, he realized, is wisdom, and wisdom starts with understanding something about understanding.

Did you know that in Jewish thinking there are three parts to wisdom? In fact the Hebrew word for it, *chabad*, is an acronym of three progressive steps.

The first step is *chokhmah* which refers to *insight*. Specifically, it represents the first flash of understanding as it is revealed to us. If one hundred people are in a room and we all hear a good idea, then *hearing* it is the first step of wisdom. Yet no matter how often we hear it, it does not make us wise.

The second step is *binah* which means discernment. It is the moment we determine if this insight is good or bad. Importantly for the context of this book, it is the moment we decide whether it is a 'God' idea and if we will act on it.

The third is *da'at*, meaning knowledge. However, knowledge in the context of wisdom is more than just information. In practice, it is a verb. *Da'at* is where we adopt insight and have acted upon it to such an extent that it is now part of us. It is where we practice the wisdom we have received until it becomes natural to us.

Da'at is where we allow God's *tupos* to turn insight into reality.

You could therefore say that the three steps of wisdom are:

> To hear.
>
> To discern.
>
> To become.

It is this second stage of wisdom that is key to momentum. *Binah* comes from the Hebrew word *beyn*, which means between and implies the ability to distinguish or discern *between* the real from the unreal, the true from the false, a God opportunity from a distraction. What marks out a wise man, therefore, is the ability to spot a connection that the foolish man does not . . . and vice versa.

In 1988, the Prime Minister of the United Kingdom declared that all public schools should have a "daily act of broadly Christian worship." Every school in the UK had to have some kind of prayer, hymn, or religious homily once a day for the entire school. Schools and teachers that felt uncomfortable fulfilling this obligation were encouraged to outsource this to those in the community. All churches in the UK heard about it (*chokhmah*), yet only a few understood the importance of the opportunity (*binah*), and so relatively few acted upon it to the point it became part of their regular church culture (*da'at*).

Most churches kept trying to grow their small internal youth groups. On the whole, we went around and around in circles, putting on events while ignoring the vast opportunities to impact our nation's youth. It is, of course, much easier to protest about the lack of God in schools than to allow God to school our methods. Sadly, most doors do not stay open permanently and a beep does not stay on the screen forever.

When Solomon asked for wisdom, he specifically asked for *binah*.

> *At Gibeon the Lord appeared to Solomon during the night in a dream, and God said, "Ask for whatever you want me to give you." Solomon answered, "[. . .] give your servant a* discerning heart *to govern your people and to distinguish between right and wrong."*[109]

Momentum as the result of *binah* can be seen in the parable of the sower. Along with the other Jewish versions of this allegory, the focus is not on the seed but on the soil in which it lands. It teaches that multiplication does not depend on the message itself but on the response of the hearer. As I said earlier, the seed may not look like the plant, taste like the plant, or smell like the plant. But so what?

It is the soil that determines if it ever will grow into the plant!

Tassels

Discernment determines whether or not we can make the link from one ring to another.

Rather than letting significant insight pass by unrealized, the Kingdom Pattern teaches us there is something for us to do . . . something we need to grasp hold of.

> *A large crowd followed and pressed around him. And a woman was there who had been subject to bleeding for twelve years. She had suffered a great deal under the care of many doctors and had spent all she had, yet instead of getting better she grew worse. When she heard about Jesus, she came up behind him*

> *in the crowd and touched his cloak, because she thought, "If I just touch his clothes, I will be healed." Immediately her bleeding stopped and she felt in her body that she was freed from her suffering.*[110]

This story is one of many great examples of *binah* in the Bible. The woman knew that if she did not get better, she would keep getting worse. She had been locked in a never ending circle of prescriptions and potions that had done nothing to help.[111] However, they had created in her the desperation she would need. A desperation that would lead Jesus to declare:

> *"Daughter, your faith has healed you. Go in faith and be freed from your suffering."*[112]

Binah led her to touch his cloak. Actually 'cloak' is not a good translation as scholars tell us that she specifically touched the tassels on the corners of his outer robe. This is surprisingly important.

The tassels had five knots, and in Jewish custom they represented the five books of the Torah with the four spaces in between representing the letters of God's name, YHWH. This may not at first appear particularly relevant, except for the fact that Malachi prophesied the Messiah would come with '*healing in his wings.*'[113] This sounds odd if you take it literally, but the Jews understood that the Hebrew word for 'wings' could also be interpreted as the tassels that Jewish men wore. Based on this, some of the Jews expected the Messiah to have healing in his tassels and some Pharisees, therefore, made them long, hoping for some kind of recognition.

Jesus said about them:

> *"Everything they do is done for people to see: They make their phylacteries wide and the tassels on their garments long."*[114]

In that crowd, many saw Jesus, many heard He was the Anointed One, and many knew the prophecy. Yet only one understood the opportunity contained a challenge. Only one discerned that a response was required. Only one was wise enough to do something with the insight she had received.

Only one reacted to the *beep*.

By touching Jesus' tassels, the woman was professing her faith in Him as the Messiah. Yet she approached Him from behind, knowing that if she had got it wrong, touching Him would make Him unclean. What a terrible thing she risked doing to a rabbi! However, by acting, she declared that she would be transformed by Him . . . not vice versa.

And she was right!

Others were sick. Others believed. Yet because she discerned that she needed to *do something*, she was freed from a static world of sickness and segregation. She had heard that Jesus was the Messiah (*chokhmah*) but before she was transformed by this knowledge (*da'at*), she first had to act on that insight (*binah*).

How many followers of Jesus are walking around in circles right now because they hear the beeps but do not understand or take the opportunity required? The Kingdom is advanced not when we do things for men to see, but when we see the things to do that other men do not.

Two thousand years ago, Jesus was the most powerful passerby of all time.

Today, He still is.

Discussion starters

1. In one of the diagrams below, put a circle around where you consider yourself to be in this Kingdom Pattern.
2. Please write down your explanation for this.
3. Is there somewhere else you would prefer to be? If so place an 'X' to mark the spot.
4. Is there an additional principle you see in the pattern that is not stated in the book?
5. Please share your thoughts on social media using: #kingdompatterns

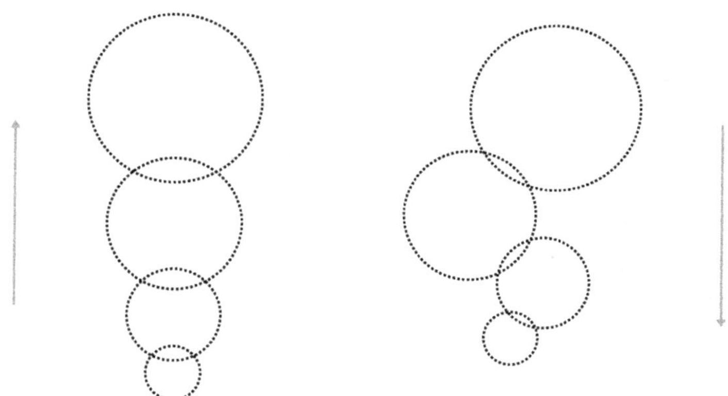

RINGS | The Pilgrim

Moses

Has anyone in history walked around in circles more than Moses?

Our hero's life demonstrates this Kingdom Pattern more than once, both in the positive and in the negative. He was highly honored by God and greatly used by Him. Yet there were key moments in his life that changed not only *his* destiny . . . but that of a nation.

We first discover Moses as a baby in a papyrus basket and at the bottom of a ring.

If you remember the story of Joseph, you will know that a small band of Abraham's descendants had fled to Egypt where, protected by Joseph, the right-hand man to Pharaoh, they had grown into a mighty nation. The problem was that four hundred years after Joseph, the Israelites were seen as a threat, and the Egyptians began to panic.

> *So they put slave masters over them to oppress them with forced labor, and they built Pithom and Rameses as store cities for Pharaoh. But the more they were oppressed, the more they multiplied and spread; so the Egyptians came to dread the Israelites and worked them ruthlessly.*[115]

After forced labor failed, they declared that all newborn Hebrew boys must be killed at birth. Moses, however, was rescued and through a bizarre set of circumstances, he entered the king's palace where he was adopted by members of the royal family and raised as a prince of Egypt.[116]

As an adult, Moses began to realize a little of who he was. A seed was placed in his heart and mind, an instinct that said he would one day be the savior of the Jews, a rescuer of sorts. Remember, however, that when such a seed is placed in our heart, we often attach it to the nearest thing we know that looks like it. Our hero fell into that same trap and, surrounded by brutality and fear, Moses sought to free his people in the ways of the world around him.

> *He saw an Egyptian beating a Hebrew, one of his own people. Looking this way and that and seeing no one, he killed the Egyptian and hid him in the sand. The next day he went out and saw two Hebrews fighting. He asked the one in the wrong, "Why are you hitting your fellow Hebrew?" The man said, "Who made you ruler and judge over us? Are you thinking of killing me as you killed the Egyptian?" Then Moses was afraid and thought, "What I did must have become known."*[117]

Moses promptly fled into a wilderness season both physically and spiritually.

What led to these tragic circumstances? Can I suggest it was entitlement? Moses had grown up in the palace of the Pharaoh. What a privilege! Yet maybe privilege was part of the problem. Joseph had gone through hell to get as close to power as Moses was by simply being born into it. Yet Joseph's pilgrimage had prepared him for that power in a way that Moses' entitlement had not. That is the problem of entitlement isn't it? We can think that a new season is owed to us. We can also think that the vision God gives us provides a license to break His laws—in Moses' case, a license to kill.

So when his opportunity came, he blew it.

God, however, is a God of grace and this Kingdom Pattern teaches us that opportunities often come around again. Each time they highlight the new season God still has for us. Yet each time they also highlight the thing He needs to change *in us* in order to enter into it. It may be something we need to train in. It may be a new character trait we need to develop, a new skill to learn, a new way of thinking.

Or perhaps it is something we need to *let go of*.

Excuses

Moses made his first connection at age eighty.

I often teach that vision does not come from the dramatic but from an awkward conversation with God. The theatrical simply gets our attention, but it is the conversation that follows which brings the purpose.

> *One day Moses was tending the flock of his father-in-law, Jethro, the priest of Midian. He led the flock far into the wilderness and came to Sinai, the mountain of God. There the angel of the Lord appeared to him in a blazing fire from the middle of a bush. Moses stared in amazement. Though the bush was engulfed in flames, it didn't burn up. "This is amazing," Moses said to himself. "Why isn't that bush burning up? I must go see it."*[118]

Moses was ready for a miracle.

More than that, he had gone from perceiving himself as the savior of his nation to the herder of sheep. Humbled and alone, not only was he ready for a miracle, he had been prepared for one.

> *"Do not come any closer," God said. "Take off your sandals, for the place where you are standing is holy ground." [. . .] At this, Moses hid his face, because he was afraid to look at God. The Lord said, "I have indeed seen the misery of my people in*

> *Egypt. I have heard them crying out because of their slave drivers, and I am concerned about their suffering . . . So now, go. I am sending you to Pharaoh to bring my people the Israelites out of Egypt."*[119]

Interestingly, when Moses was on *holy ground,* he got to the very place many of us would love to be. He reached the utopia of worship. He felt a strong sense of God's presence all around and God spoke directly to him. Imagine that. Is that not the end goal? To enter God's presence and never leave?

Yet within moments, God said:

> *"Go."*

Our end goals are nothing more than God's rest stops. God is a God who brings momentum.

> *But Moses said to God, "Who am I that I should go to Pharaoh and bring the Israelites out of Egypt?"*[120]

The first excuse of Moses revealed what God had done in him over the last forty years. He felt like a nobody. The pride that had hindered him so many years ago was less evident. Not only that, but he understood something else:

> *Moses said to God, "Suppose I go to the Israelites and say to them, 'The God of your fathers has sent me to you,' and they ask me, 'What is his name?' Then what shall I tell them?"*[121]

Moses realized he did not have all the answers and although raised as a prince, he felt unequipped for what God was asking of him.

> *Moses said to the LORD, "O Lord, I have never been eloquent, neither in the past nor since you have spoken to your servant. I am slow of speech and tongue."*[122]

Moses' ultimate conclusion was seen when he simply said:

"Lord, please send someone else."[123]

Moses was full of excuses. Yet he made the connection.

Then Moses went back to Jethro his father-in-law and said to him, "Let me return to my own people . . ."[124]

He had received *insight* in a miracle but *discernment* through a conversation.

In that awkward conversation with God, Moses expressed many good reasons for not doing what he needed to do. Yet his excuses helped him discover a way forward. They led him to understand that with God all things are possible if we do all things His way. His excuses were a result of fear—the fear of failure that he learned by missing his previous opportunity. His excuses were also what led him to uncover God's truth.

Excuses can be your servant, but you must never become their slave.

Wilderness

Moses moved forward and brought momentum to an entire nation.

After much debate with Pharaoh and many signs and wonders, the Israelites left Egypt on their way to an unknown country. However, all Kingdom Patterns repeat themselves, and so on the border of the land that God had vowed to give them, we again see our pilgrim face another link in the chain of life.

Just before Moses and the Israelites were about to enter the Promised Land, he inexplicably sent spies to explore the territory ahead of them. The surprise was not that he commissioned them, but that he made their names public and turned their discoveries into a discussion.

They gave Moses this account: "We went into the land to which you sent us, and it does flow with milk and honey! Here is its

> *fruit. But the people who live there are powerful, and the cities are fortified and very large."*[125]

This was a disastrous and defining moment in Israel's history.

Moses held a debate to discuss whether or not to do something God had already told him to do. Why would you do that? Maybe so others can talk you out of it? Maybe so you can hide your will behind *their* decision? For whichever reason, after successfully making the connection with God's plan when called out of Egypt, Moses now he failed to link up with the next ring when called into the Promised Land.

And this was the result:

> *"For forty years—one year for each of the forty days you explored the land—you will suffer for your sins and know what it is like to have me against you."*[126]

Can you imagine that? To have God *against* you for forty years! What did that look like? Well, the journey to the Promised Land should have taken them a couple of weeks; instead it took forty years. That's an average speed of six miles per year! Yet they did not walk in slow motion, did they? They did not follow the same path but only at a snail's pace. No, they carried on going around and around in circles.[127]

It would take another season of forty years for the Hebrew nation to rediscover momentum. Not only would the obvious culture of non-appreciation need to be replaced in a new generation, but God would have to take them on a forty year journey of signs and wonders, because sadly that was what was required to rebuild their faith.

Could it be that the journey you are on right now is rebuilding your faith?

If so, the quicker it grows, the sooner you will be ready for your next link.

Pharaoh

Jesus is the way, but the devil creates waywardness.

> *For the waywardness of the simple will kill them, and the complacency of fools will destroy them!*[128]

The horror movies that frighten Satan are the word pictures painted by Jesus and populated by Kingdom-possessed people. So rather than help you move upward, the devil will attempt to bring you down by causing you to miss God's connections. He will offer you something good if it stops you from doing something great. He will lead you downwards and, importantly, shrink your boundaries.

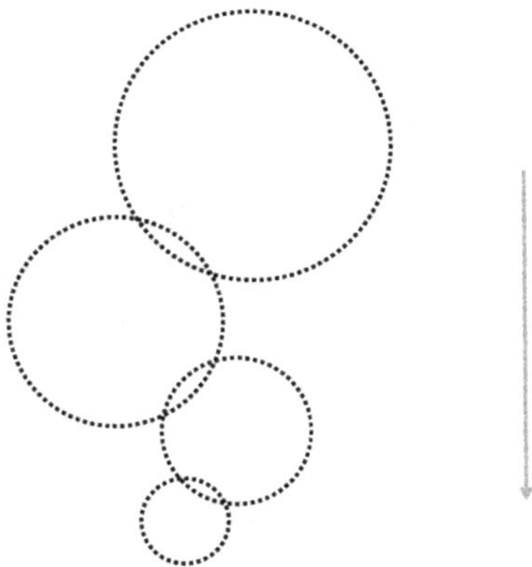

However, your enemy has a problem, and it is not what you think.

Occasionally, I hear Christians labeling the devil as foolish or dense or idiotic. I have even heard Christians tell of their amazement that Satan does not know his future. But they are wrong.

He is not stupid. He is a slave.

He *does* know his future. His problem is not that he doesn't know what he is doing, but that he cannot help himself. The devil is much smarter than you or I, but he is a sinner who has become the greatest of all slaves to sin. We know he will be eternally punished because we know his heart is eternally hardened.

His predicament, however, gives us an insight into the negative possibilities of this pattern:

> *The magicians could not stand before Moses because of the boils that were on them and on all the Egyptians. But the Lord hardened Pharaoh's heart and he would not listen . . .* [129]

Stop right there.

The *Lord* hardened Pharaoh's heart? I have a problem with that. In fact, I have several problems with that. For a start: How can God call Himself a loving God when He hardens someone's heart? Also, what about free will? And anyway, why does God choose to harden some people's hearts and not others?

Although I would love to dismiss this verse as an unfortunate turn of phrase, I cannot. You see, it is not an isolated incident. There are forty-six references in the Bible to God intervening in this way.[130] The fact is that God does actively, purposely, and with forethought harden people's hearts.

There is a three step process to this that appears to shadow the three steps of wisdom:

> We hear.
>
> We *disregard*.
>
> We become.

Pharaoh's story provides a classic case study of how God hardens hearts and shows the three potential steps in the negative version of this Kingdom Pattern.

Step #1: God says He will.

God knew Pharaoh's heart and the struggle he was having with God's request, and He warned Moses that He would harden Pharaoh's heart.[131]

To help us understand this battle of wills, we need to grasp some of its context.

> *Then a new king, to whom Joseph meant nothing, came to power in Egypt. "Look," he said to his people, "the Israelites have become far too numerous for us. Come, we must deal shrewdly with them or they will become even more numerous and, if war breaks out, will join our enemies, fight against us and leave the country."*[132]

That passage contains a self-fearfilling prophecy.

Well before the meeting with Moses, the king of Egypt had fear in his heart. Ironically, when this happens to us, the things we put in place to avoid our worst nightmare are often the very things that end up bringing that bad dream into reality. So Pharaoh's ethnic cleansing was bizarrely what led to the rise of his nemesis.

Due to his actions, six hundred thousand adult Hebrew men left Egypt with Moses, plus an unspecified but apparently large number of non-Hebrews as well.

> *"A mixed multitude also went up with them."*[133]

It's been estimated that, including women and children, two million people fled Egypt. This is a significant number when you consider that historians suggest that the entire population of Egypt at that time was somewhere between three and four million and definitely not higher than six million. Moses was not asking Pharaoh to release a small tribe of people; he was requesting permission for around a third of the population to go with him!

Pharaoh was not simply struggling with the question: *"Is this God?"* He *heard* God's warning. He was defeated by the temptation to ignore it.

Step #2: We harden our hearts.

Before God hardened Pharaoh's heart, Pharaoh hardened it first!

> *"But when Pharaoh saw that there was relief, he hardened his heart and would not listen to Moses and Aaron, just as the Lord had said."*[134]

The word used here for hardening can mean calloused and 'fat as grease.' This represents the numbing effect of sin when we no longer feel the pain of hurting God's heart.

The more we continue in our sin, the less we feel.

Or you could say:

> The less often we change, the easier it is to change less often.

Step #3: God hardens our hearts.

Why?

Athletes work hard to keep their body supple; if not, they will easily be broken. God would prefer our spirits to be supple; but if not, He will break us. So to do this He must first harden our hearts. When our hearts are hardened, this leads us to make really bad choices that often culminate in sending us to the pit of despair. However, being in that pit is often what it takes to cause us to finally repent. But even if we do not, we become a warning sign to those who might otherwise follow us.

Either way, God's way is glorified.

> *"But I will make Pharaoh's heart stubborn so I can multiply my miraculous signs and wonders in the land of Egypt."*[135]

The wonderful thing about this Kingdom Pattern is that no matter where you find yourself, an opportunity will once again come around for you to connect with His next season. Your life can wind upwards once again.

You see, with God, the most important thing is not where you are, but which way you are going.

Now, how exciting is that!

Discussion starters

Please take a look at these incidents from Moses' life. Then put the number for each one where you think he was on this Kingdom Pattern.

1. Moses kills an Egyptian and flees to Midian: Exodus 2:12-15
2. Moses meets God at the burning bush: Exodus 3:1-3
3. Moses makes the decision to go to Pharaoh: Exodus 4:18
4. Moses holds a debate: Numbers 13:26
5. Moses told the people they will not enter the land for 40 years: Numbers 14:34
6. Moses dishonors God: Numbers 27:12-14

What is a key principle you see in Moses' ring-shaped journey?

Please share the principle on social media using: #kingdompatterns

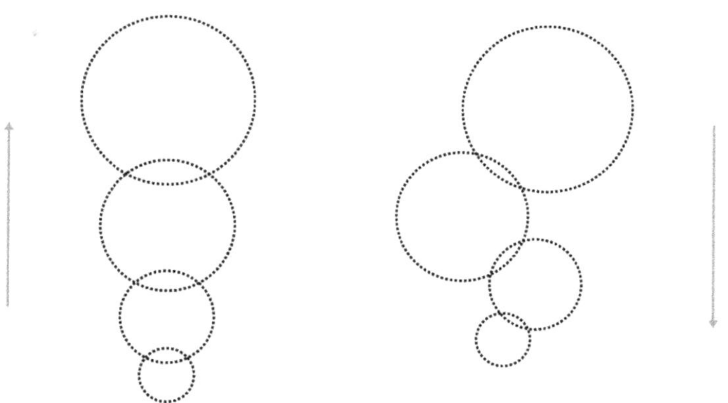

RINGS | The Practices

Christmas

Practice #1: *Prepare today for tomorrow's opportunity will come!*

Prepare your heart. Prepare your mind. Prepare your question.

God's plan for your life is not to lead you with a carrot on the end of a stick. He only offers what can be attained. In fact, it is true to say that God has not hidden things *from* you but *for* you.

When my two sons were at the age where they were very excited about receiving Christmas presents, they would often ask my wife the same questions many times over. "Can I have this? Can I have that?"

One day my eldest son pleaded, almost begged, for a remote controlled car, not knowing that one already lay hidden three feet away, under the sofa. It was being saved for the right time and when he was in the right attitude to receive it. On Christmas Day, when he had awoken and had prayed his thanksgiving prayer, he would excitedly rip open the wrapping and play with it.

It was hidden not *from him*, but *for him.*

Any vision that God has placed on your heart is not being used to simply motivate you. It is hidden for you, awaiting the moment you are ready for it. The sooner you notice the beeps, the sooner you change what must be changed, the sooner you will make the connection and enter into that new season.

But why the delay?

There may be several reasons for this, but I have found one common principle.

It has a lot to do with the achievement of God's dreams, not just yours. It could even be the reason that you may be going around in circles right now. The goal of all the Kingdom Patterns is that your primary question for finding direction becomes: "What is the most effective thing I can do for His Kingdom?" Until then, direction may be hidden from you until it does more good than bad, and when it leads you to a greater vision of Him, not a greater vision of vision.

Put simply:

> God will not give to you what will become *God* to you.

Code

Practice #2: *Listen to the white noise!*

Be aware of it. Be listening for it. Be tuned in to it.

Our lives are full of clichés. A cliché can be defined as something once profound but losing its effectiveness due to overuse.

There is a story told of a man who went for an interview to be a Morse Code operator. Entering the noisy office of his prospective employer, he was led to a waiting room where six other nervous applicants were already seated. There was one other door apart from the one he had just entered. The sign on it read 'Manager.'

None of the seven applicants talked to each other due to the loud clattering of telegraph machines, raised voices, ringing phones, and other competing sounds. After five minutes however, much to the astonishment of the other men, the seventh applicant stood up and boldly walked through into the manager's office. Two minutes later, the executive led him back out into the waiting room and with a sympathetic tone said to those who had been sitting patiently, "Thank you, but the position has now been taken by this gentleman."

The other six applicants were astonished and upset. Their indignation was apparent when they immediately complained that they had not been given a chance to interview—until, that is, they received the following reply: "Actually our process was as fair as we could possibly make it, for the past five minutes a message in Morse Code has been filling the air, stating that the first person to walk into the manager's office would get the job."

They all heard the message, but it had become background noise to them.

The very thing that you are asking God to reveal to you may be the very thing He has been saying to you all along. It may be that it sounds too simple because you have heard it so often. The sad irony is that the very thing God uses to lead us towards His goal is the very thing that can lead us to ignore it: repetition.

What have you heard God say so often that it has become background noise to you?

Gremlins

Practice #3: *Don't ignore your weaknesses!*

Recognize them. Be realistic about them. Be prepared to regulate them.

There are many things that make you adorable. Oddly, some of them are your faults. Maybe you are cutely forgetful. Perhaps people smile when you turn up a little late because it is just "so you." Perhaps you are a real stickler for things being in order. These quirks can be attractive. This week for instance, my team put up a row of clocks on the wall, each one representing the time in a nation where Pais serves. Then they took bets as to how long it would take for a returning German team member to notice the second hands were slightly out of sync with each other and waste endless amounts of time to correct them. Sometimes his idiosyncrasies drive them crazy, but mostly they love him for them.

In the 1980's film 'Gremlins,' the world was plagued by a lot of furry little creatures that were cute and adorable . . . until they touched water. At that point they then became destructive flesh-eating monsters.

It has been pointed out that our weaknesses are just like that.[136]

The faults that make you, well, *you* are endearing . . . until they come into contact with your calling. At that point, they become destructive, vision-eating monsters, and you need to deal with them. If you do not, then potentially the things your friends love about you may cause you to miss the next season God has for you.

As you go around and around in a never ending circle, one of the beeps you might hear may be highlighting a weakness. A fault of yours that in the past was never a major issue for you, but one that God knows will prevent you from succeeding in a new season.

One of the best leaders of our movement used to be the nicest person on the planet. Everyone knew him to be gracious, encouraging, and forgiving to a fault, *literally*. The problem came when part of his new role was to interview applicants. At that point, his kindness and desire to see everyone be given an opportunity almost ruined more than one team. He accepted people who should have never been given a place on Pais, and the team they joined then paid for his mistake.

What made him quite popular as a person made him a nightmare as a leader.

To his great credit, however, against his second nature, he changed. Seeing the repeated issues arising in teams prompted him to gain control of his naivety. He led Pais in his nation into a new season and it has continued to flourish since that time.

Sadly, however, Moses never completely conquered *his* weaknesses. Therefore, tragically, he never entered the Promised Land.

> *Then Moses raised his arm and struck the rock twice with his staff. Water gushed out, and the community and their livestock drank. But the Lord said to Moses and Aaron, "Because you did not trust in me enough to honor me as holy in the sight of the Israelites, you will not bring this community into the land I give them."*[137]

The reason God was so angry with Moses has never been completely pin-pointed. But, it is widely agreed that Moses was angry with the Israelites when he did not need to be. They were simply asking for water. This anger came from frustration in what God had called him to do and the position it put him in.

At times this frustration led to him to say to the people, *"Shall we bring you forth water?"* instead of *"Shall God bring you forth water?"* Then when asked by God to *speak* to the rock, he instead *struck* it and, in doing so, brought attention to himself as the people's savior rather than to God.

It is this fault in Moses that helps us see his human side. His weaknesses enable us to relate to someone who may otherwise seem super-human. His flaws help us to connect to his story. It is this victim mentality, however, that also acted as an anchor and caused him to miss his ultimate connection.

My personal belief is that God's barring of Moses was not simply retrospective punishment but a pro-active protection from the damage Moses' frustration might have created in the Promised Land.

No one is perfect and you may never be excellent in your areas of weakness. Yet this Kingdom Pattern highlights our faults in order to give us an opportunity to work through them. Recognizing where we are in the pattern can lead us to a place where they no longer provide such a threat. Managing them will not make us more special to God, but they will enable us to become more strategic to Him.

So do not ignore your weaknesses, even if your friends do.

Hype

Practice #4: *Don't dismiss the hype!*

Use it. Don't abuse it. And don't confuse it with false promises.

There is a right time to connect. Miss it, and someone else may make the connection instead.

God sowed His Word into the Jews, but its many blessings were harvested by the Gentiles. God promised a land to the followers of Moses, but those who followed Joshua are the ones that entered into it.

> *They gave Moses this account: "We went into the land to which you sent us, and it does flow with milk and honey! Here is its fruit. [. . .]" Then Caleb silenced the people before Moses and said, "We should go up and take possession of the land, for we can certainly do it."*[138]

Caleb had passion and when I read this verse, I imagine him pleading God's case with every charismatic bone in his body. Yet I am sure Caleb's enthusiastic description was seen as mere hype.

Joshua, however, bought into it.

Two of the spies may have given a good report, but negativity finds it easy to disguise itself as wisdom and positivity sadly can appear to be foolish hype. We therefore dismiss hype because of its negative connotation. It conjures up the idea of something being masqueraded for more than it is, something too good to be true, but that is not what hype means. Hype has a purpose. Its very definition means to stimulate, liven, and increase.

Why does God encourage the use of music in our worship of Him? Because the dynamic of worship stimulates us. In that sense, music is a tool of hype. There is a reason it is played at the end of a sermon or during a climactic moment in a movie. It trumps our doubts and fears.

Hype creates a tipping point.

It causes us to make a commitment that we might never make in the cold light of the day. It increases, livens, and stimulates our faith to make the sacrifice or change we may need to make. Hype comes in many formats—the passionate preacher, the persuasive leader, the spine-tingling divine appointment, the heart-stopping God-incidence, plus many others. When partnered with the repeated beeps, it can wind you upwards.

Can I encourage you to allow hype to do its job? Grasp an opportunity when it arises. Give it permission to push you further than you've gone before. Take hold of the opportunity that God is providing *when* He provides it. Do not simply acknowledge that the opportunity is before you . . . because it may not always be.

As the riddle goes, there were three frogs sitting on a lily pad and *two* decided to jump off. How many frogs were left sitting on the lilypad?

Three.

Two only *decided* to jump off.

Discussion starters

Practice #1: *Prepare today for tomorrow's opportunity will come!*
Practice #2: *Listen to the white noise!*
Practice #3: *Don't ignore your weaknesses!*
Practice #4: *Don't dismiss the hype!*

1. Which of these practices seems most relevant to you at this point in your journey?
2. What is the next practical step for you to take?
3. What questions do you still have?
4. What advice that I have not written would you give someone journeying on this pattern?
5. Please share your questions and advice on social media using: #kingdompatterns

KINGDOM PATTERN

TRENCH

TRENCH | The Pattern

Approval

Confirmation is trench-shaped.

One obstacle in finding God's direction is that we look for validation from others.

This, of course, is not altogether wrong; noticing whether we are really gifted in encouragement, communication, healing, and so on will of course be reflected in the impact we have on others. If I think I am a pastor but no one feels cared for by me, then it is unlikely I am a pastor.

However, the problem occurs when we look for recognition in the things people can give: *status*, *resources*, *finance*, *titles*. These are often the confirmation tools we long for and are affirmed by, but they are false indicators when seeking God's direction.

Many years ago a key long-term member of Pais approached me to ask if we could no longer refer to her as a 'Pais worker' but as a 'staff member.' Apparently she was being teased by a church minister due to her title. Others struggled with the need for approval, not because we were paid so little, but because our low incomes made our work seem less valuable to friends and family. You see, something harmful happens when our decision to follow God's path is unduly influenced by the need for people's recognition. The question "Lord, what is the most *effective* thing I could do for Your Kingdom?" is replaced with "Friends, what is the most *validated* thing I can do for His Kingdom?"

In my first book, I mentioned how I was viewed by one senior Christian more highly as the pastor of a small church of nineteen people than the leader of a work reaching tens of thousands of high school students. When this kind of thing happens, it tests our motives. In fact, several times in my life God seemed to be purposely making it difficult for me to serve Him. Maybe this is part of a filtering process. Could it be that, rather than hampering my work as it seemed, He was instead purifying my motives for doing it?

This would actually make sense because He has a Kingdom Pattern for just that!

You would think that your effort would be equal to your recognition, wouldn't you? The harder you work, the greater influence you should have, and the greater the influence you have, the larger the recognition you should receive. These elements should surely run parallel to each other, right?

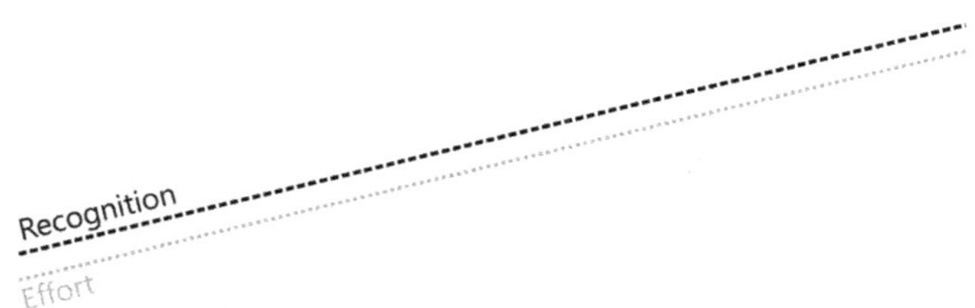

Instead, the repeated pattern we see may look very different, because the connection between effort and recognition is affected by time.

Simply put, there are three parts to this pattern.

Midgleys

At first, things are done *for you*.

In this first stage, you are recognized for standing out because you have a passion for something that others may not. People are happy for you and get behind you. A spotlight may even shine on you for a little time. Not that many questions are asked about what you are doing and how you are doing it, because people are just glad someone is doing something!

At this point you may strongly feel 'the hand of God on your life' because people are celebrating and encouraging you, even blessing you with some practical help. The circumstances point to you being on the right path every time you are applauded and resourced for stepping out.

However, the recognition you receive is actually disproportionate to the success you are achieving.

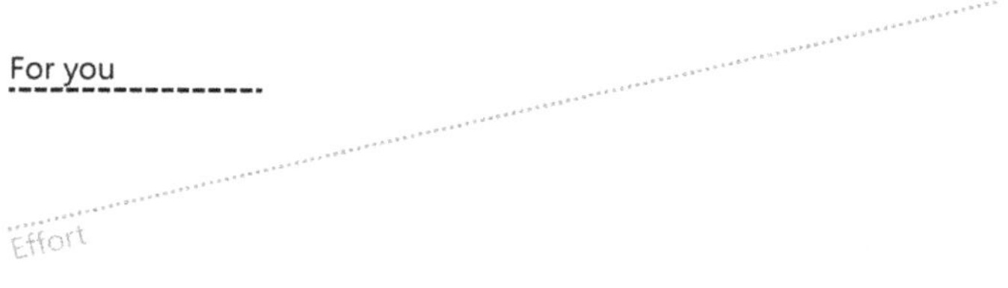

You see, the resources which flow so early lead us to believe our personal efforts are responsible for having a greater impact than they really do.

When Pais apprentices join the Pais Project as part of our youth leader apprenticeship, they have not as yet earned the right to speak in the schools they enter. They have not spent three years in a teacher training college but are instead piggybacking on the reputation of Pais. This principle is also true of our Pais Venture and Pais Collective apprentices who work with businesses and churches respectively. The initial success they see is partly due to the materials, infrastructure, training, and sustenance provided for them. You see, for a seed to gain a good start in life, it is often planted by the gardener in an artificially supportive environment, such as a greenhouse. This is required because, as the ad agency entrepreneur William Bernbach once pointed out:

> For a flower to blossom, you need the right soil as well as the right seed.[139]

However, that environment not only speeds up the growth process of the seed, it also protects it from the reality of harsher conditions. Only once that seed is transplanted into a more usual environment, does its real qualities become evident.

To be honest, I think most of our apprentices understand this; however, some outside the organization may not. This is clear to see when a church hires a Pais apprentice but does not provide the same infrastructure. Note Bernbach's further observation:

> I'm amused when other agencies try to hire my people away [and get the same results]. They'd have to 'hire' the whole environment.

So in this first part of the pattern, our success is not our own. It is provided for us.

When I first stepped into my calling to reach schools, I did not make the biggest sacrifice. Others did. My pastor forfeited a portion of his wages so that the church could pay me a small salary. The schools opened up because of the service we offered, but the ground had been softened by churches who had given free books to their libraries for years. Although it cost Lynn and me to keep our apprenticeship free for others, a Christian businessman supplemented our finances so we could have a summer vacation.

Then there were those who went the extra mile.

In the early nineties, Pete and Helen Midgley were a young married couple who financially supported me in the work I did. In fact, they

were so committed to it that Helen took on a second job to raise more money for the family in order that they could fund me to a greater degree! They cared about me and the vision into which I was stepping.

However, as I said in the first book of this trilogy, some people may believe in *you* but not necessarily in *it*.

Herein lies the problem and the inevitable journey into 'the trench.'

Trap

In the second stage of this pattern, things are done *by you*.

One day you will turn around and realize you are 'old news.' You are no longer the shining light, the new kid on the block, the next big thing. Suddenly your journey does not grab the limelight in the same way it used to do. You have just become part of the furniture. In fact, people may not understand exactly what it is you are doing or why you are doing it that way. So, as you move deeper into the purpose God has given you, the resources and, in particular, the recognition do not necessarily follow in the way you might expect.

Essentially, you go underground.

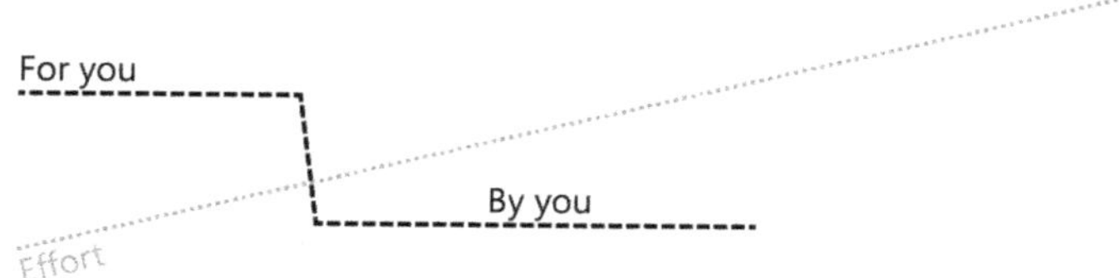

As your dreams gain momentum, they will require more resources such as time, energy, money, and so on, but the recognition of others may not increase at the same rate. Sadly, some of us may mistake this to mean that God is no longer involved.

This is the problem when confirmation comes from an artificial source.

From my viewpoint, the Pais Movement is in the trench and is therefore not seen by some for what it truly is. We reach so many people at so little cost at such a formative time in their lives and yet far fewer people join or give support than I would expect. I am sure you will go through this at some point as well. You will find that you have to make the choice between what is the most effective thing you can do and what is the most commonly accepted thing you can do.

This is a normal pattern for those following God's direction and God uses this process to refine your motives for following His dreams. I have seen this happen to me several times, and I am therefore no longer disappointed when it happens again.

I do, however, have a confession to make. I used to have a *secret fantasy*.

For several years, I would lay awake at night role-playing my embarrassing dream in my imagination. It went like this: through no fault of my own, Pais would die! I imagined the prime minister of the UK creating some kind of legislation that, in effect, outlawed our work. I would then turn to the people around me and say, "Sadly we have to finish. I really want to carry on, but what can I do?" Then with a Gallic shrug, I would walk away.

This secret fantasy was the result of the burden I felt during the early days of Pais. After all, if I understood the Bible correctly, without the work we were doing, some young people would go to a forever without God! Yet I realized that if I gave up, there was not enough recognition of its importance to be taken up by someone else. How tragic is that! You walk away and the impact you had, the help you gave others, the inspiration you brought simply goes away with you. Self-pity would well up in me when we were given little financial

support or promotional opportunities. It kept asking me the question: why are you doing this?

This season of my life lasted for some years. However, those days are now gone. I no longer have that fantasy, because I have grown to understand something that ironically empowers me:

The trench is a *trap*.

If you pursue God's direction in your life by constantly asking yourself and God the question, "What is the most effective thing I can do to advance the Kingdom of God?" then you may also find yourself in a similar position, committed to a path you also feel constrained by. There might be times when you simply 'want out,' but the fact that no one else will do what you do forces you to stick at it.

During that time, the *tupos* of God will repeatedly demolish the need for personal recognition. The purpose of this pattern is to destroy the rut of looking for confirmation in other things. Instead, it will cut a new channel: the desire to simply do what God loves you to do.

The trench is a trap, but it is also a tool.

Iconic

In the third stage of this pattern, things are done *because of you*.

Something magical happens when you stick at something for so long that people forget about you: eventually, when they remember you, what you are doing has become almost legendary.

I first noticed this with pop stars.

When I was younger, ABBA, Johnny Cash, Tom Jones, and other musicians had some initial fame and then quickly became old-fashioned. They became somewhat forgettable—you knew their music was still around but it was no longer very popular other than among their most ardent fans. Years later, however, they suddenly became 'legends in their own lifetime,' and no matter how at odds their particular brand of music was to the current scene, they were seen as superstars . . . icons.

I think there is something about sticking at what you believe in, no matter how unappreciated it may be, that not only builds inward *character* but outward *charisma*.
At this stage, things become more effective.

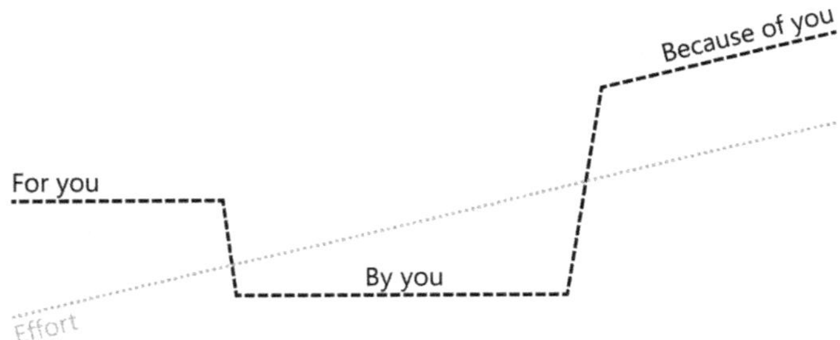

In fact, the personal work you do has an even greater impact than it should! People recognize your endeavor because it is something that is proven. It is proven not by your commitment to success, but to the trench. The trench proves you believe in what you say you believed in. They know that if they invest in you, believe in you, partner with you (marry you), you are not going to give up when things get tough, because you didn't. Therefore, people not only recognize what you are doing, but because of what you have been through, they partner with you to a much higher degree than before.

This results in a far greater impact than you previously had.

Your words have more power than they previously would have, your requests have more weight that they normally should have, and your presentations have more status than they previously could have.

One day, I believe Pais will come out of the trench. I look forward to it because it means we will inspire many others to do similar but greater things, and our effectiveness will be multiplied.

Going through your trench has still one more advantage. It shows people that they can get through theirs. It gives people hope. People want to be where you are, and now they know what it takes to get there. After all, a hero is not a hero because of *their* courage but because of the courage they give to *others*.

Now who does that make me think of?

Discussion starters

1. Put a circle around where you consider yourself to be in this Kingdom Pattern.
2. Please write down your explanation for this.
3. Is there somewhere else you would prefer to be? If so place an 'X' to mark the spot.
4. Is there an additional principle you see in the pattern that is not stated in the book?
5. Please share your thoughts on social media using: #kingdompatterns

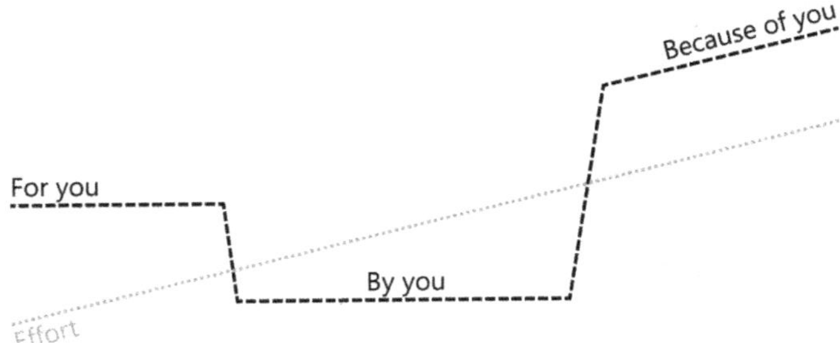

TRENCH | The Pilgrim

Nehemiah

There once was a man who gave people the boldness to build a trench in enemy territory.

Not only that, but his pilgrimage put the fear of God into his adversaries and created a story so inspiring that it has motivated humans for thousands of years. It all started, however, with a bit of bad news:

> *Hanani, one of my brothers, came from Judah with some other men, and I questioned them about the Jewish remnant that had survived the exile, and also about Jerusalem. They said to me, "Those who survived the exile and are back in the province are in great trouble and disgrace. The wall of Jerusalem is broken down, and its gates have been burned with fire." When I heard these things, I sat down and wept.*[140]

You see, the account actually hurt Nehemiah. I don't mean he was just annoyed or simply disappointed by it. He was tangibly burdened by it.

> If you can tolerate something, you cannot change it.[141]

Unlike others actually living in Jerusalem, Nehemiah could not tolerate the situation there, and so he would have to change it! This meant more than just having a meltdown or throwing a tantrum on social media. It meant doing something that others would dismiss as crazy and pointless. It meant returning to Jerusalem and rebuilding a wall in the middle of a hostile environment.

First, however, he needed to get someone to do something *for him*.

Canary

Providentially, Nehemiah was the king's canary.

Canaries are little yellow birds from Africa. They were used as an early warning system by coal miners to alert them to a poisonous gas leak. Canaries would be the first to die if carbon monoxide was filling the air. In a similar way, one of Nehemiah's duties was to test the wine in advance of his master in case of an assassination attempt. This meant he was in the king's presence on a daily basis. The role also required a trustworthy character and, according to historians, a sunny disposition. This helped Nehemiah get noticed.

> *In the month of Nisan in the twentieth year of King Artaxerxes, when wine was brought for him, I took the wine and gave it to the king. I had not been sad in his presence before, so the king asked me, "Why does your face look so sad when you are not ill? This can be nothing but sadness of heart."*[142]

It was Nehemiah's passion that got attention. He wanted permission to do something that Artaxerxes had previously banned the Jews from doing and therefore had not been asked of him since![143]

> *I was very much afraid, but I said to the king, "May the king live forever! Why should my face not look sad when the city where my ancestors are buried lies in ruins, and its gates have been destroyed by fire?" The king said to me, "What is it you want?" Then I prayed to the God of heaven, and I answered the king, "If it pleases the king and if your servant has found favor in his sight, let him send me to the city in Judah where my ancestors are buried so that I can rebuild it." [. . .] And because*

> *the gracious hand of my God was on me, the king granted my requests.*[144]

The king not only granted Nehemiah's request but what he did next was huge!

> *So I went to the governors of Trans-Euphrates and gave them the king's letters. The king had also sent army officers and cavalry with me.*[145]

When God's servant returned to Jerusalem, he did not go as a lowly wine-taster, but as one with great authority. Authority had been given him that would make his work far more impactful than it normally would have been.

Nehemiah's initial success was provided *for him*.

Reputation

His triumph, however, did not last long.

> *When Sanballat heard that we were rebuilding the wall, he became angry and was greatly incensed. He ridiculed the Jews, and in the presence of his associates and the army of Samaria, he said, "What are those feeble Jews doing? Will they restore their wall? Will they offer sacrifices? Will they finish in a day? Can they bring the stones back to life from those heaps of rubble—burned as they are?" Tobiah the Ammonite, who was at his side, said, "What they are building—even a fox climbing up on it would break down their wall of stones!"*[146]

Sanballat was the governor of Samaria, and Tobiah was from a family of well-known Jewish aristocrats. Neither of them were just annoying backseat critics with little influence; they were men of significance. To combat Nehemiah and protect their own interests, they used their power to convince the people of two things: firstly, that Nehemiah's task was impossible, and secondly, that he had ulterior motives.

For some of us, the opinion of well-respected people can lead us to give up on what we know for sure. However, although Nehemiah did not receive the recognition or adulation of those that mattered, he continued to do the right thing simply because it was the right thing.

In doing so, Nehemiah entered a trench.

First, an open letter from his enemies implied that Nehemiah would crown himself king once the wall was built.[147] Secondly, another rumor was spread by a man hired to trick Nehemiah into hiding in a certain part of the temple where, as a layman, he was not allowed to be and would have been viewed as a sinner if he had done so. Thirdly, false prophets had risen up to claim God was against him. Everything was aimed to undermine his credibility and the credibility of what he was doing.

Yet Nehemiah's blunt, straight-forward answer to his critics made me smile:

> *Nothing like what you are saying is happening; you are just making it up out of your head.*[148]

Nehemiah, knowing the truth, stayed on course. He understood something important that would later be said by Jesus:

> *No one who puts his hand to the plow and then looks back is fit for the kingdom of God.*[149]

After all, the trench is a trap, and the only other option was to give up.

To Nehemiah, that was no option at all!

He knew that if the wall continued to lie in ruins, then to some extent so would God's reputation. So, not only would Nehemiah need to rebuild Jerusalem's walls, he would need to help to rebuild its character as well. Non-believers everywhere were watching God's children intently, and Nehemiah was acutely aware of this. Yet the 'nobles' clearly did not care. They were in it for what they could get out of it. As the exiles returned and borrowed money to do God's work, the nobles lent them money and used it to take advantage of them. You see, some of the Jewish leaders were both taking land from Jews and also enslaving Jewish daughters when their debts could not be paid.

While in the trench, Nehemiah had been buying those Jews back out of slavery and feeding them. He confronted the nobles and corrected their practices for various reasons, but one that is explicitly stated stands out in the text:

> *So I continued, "What you are doing is not right. Shouldn't you walk in the fear of our God to avoid the reproach of our Gentile enemies?"*[150]

If you want to enrage a man or woman who loves Jesus, do something to embarrass God.

Nehemiah, like all great Biblical leaders, such as David when seeing Goliath or Jesus when seeing the money-changers at the temple, was filled with rage at anything that would harm the reputation of God in front of non-believers. In his pilgrimage, Nehemiah had allowed God's dream to become his dream, and the evidence of this was that he cared more about his master's reputation than his own.

Perhaps this is the sign to help us recognize if God's *tupos* is having its affect in our lives:

> Are we beginning to think more highly of God's good name than our own?

Nehemiah was alone in his integrity because he was alone in his *conviction* of what needed to be done. Yet rather than complain or see the lack of provision as 'God closing the door,' he kept his principles to the point where Josephus the historian said of him:

> *Nehemiah himself made the rounds of the city by night, never tiring either through work or lack of food and sleep, neither of which he took for pleasure but out of necessity.*[151]

Yet the most surprising thing about Nehemiah's story lies elsewhere.

Hidden

Nehemiah chapter eleven divulges a shocking fact.

Noticed what happened *after* the wall was reconstructed:

> *Now the leaders of the people settled in Jerusalem. The rest of the people cast lots to bring one out of every ten of them to live in Jerusalem, the holy city, while the remaining nine were to stay in their own towns.*[152]

Once the people had rebuilt the wall, no one wanted to live there!

In fact, the people commended all those who actually volunteered to live in Jerusalem because the vast majority refused to do the same, primarily for economic reasons.[153] Can you imagine being in that situation where even the people helping you do not want to fully live in that vision?

Nehemiah is famous for building something physical, tangible, and in plain sight. Yet perhaps the greatest lesson we can learn from his story is hidden. So hidden, in fact, that the Bible does not record it. Fortunately, however, the Roman historian Josephus does:

> *Nehemiah, seeing that the city had a small population, urged the priests and the Levites to leave the countryside and move to the city and remain there, for he had prepared houses for them at his own expense.*[154]

Nehemiah was in the trench and while he was, he had to pay for God's dream himself!

That's a great lesson to learn—if you want to know if a vision is from God or not, then ask, "Will I have to pay for my part in it?" If the answer is no, then I would suggest you treat it with some skepticism.

We can also learn a significant lesson about God's direction from the Jews in and around Jerusalem. Sometimes we can love a vision more than we are prepared to live in it. We can fall in love with certain ideas and be prepared to fight for them, but the question is: Do we actually want to live according to them once they become real? It is an important question because if we are not prepared to live in our beliefs, then we essentially declare them meaningless to us.

Sometimes we have little idea of what the big idea really means!

No wonder Jesus warned us not to construct something without first finding out if we could afford to build it. Might I add: and then *live in it.*

This Kingdom Pattern forces us to experience the reality of our vision, not our daydreams. It helps us come to terms with its cost. That cost purifies our motives. It asks us if we really believe something to the point of doing it without the recognition or the resources of others.

It tells us that at some point, we have to inhabit our inspirations.

Fifty-Two

Incredibly, the wall was rebuilt in fifty-two days!

> *So the wall was completed on the twenty-fifth of Elul, in fifty-two days. When all our enemies heard about this, all the surrounding nations were afraid and lost their self-confidence, because they realized that this work had been done with the help of our God.*[155]

Due to the "healing of the wall" as the Jewish Tanakh puts it, the people were gathered together and saw something worth celebrating! Finally, everyone began to understand why Nehemiah did what he did.

Nehemiah exited the trench.

Not only that, but the physical rebuilding of the wall galvanized the Jews spiritually as well.

> *All the people came together as one in the square before the Water Gate. They told Ezra the teacher of the Law to bring out the Book of the Law of Moses, which the Lord had commanded for Israel [. . .] And all the people listened attentively to the Book of the Law. [. . .] They stood in their places and confessed their sins and the sins of their ancestors [. . .] "In all that has happened to us, you have remained righteous; you have acted faithfully, while we acted wickedly."*[156]

Months earlier, Nehemiah had wept because the Jews had left the city in ruins. Now, he not only saw *them* weep at their wickedness, but he had to actually cheer them up!

> *Then Nehemiah the governor, Ezra the priest and teacher of the Law, and the Levites who were instructing the people said to them all, "This day is holy to the Lord your God. Do not mourn or weep." For all the people had been weeping as they listened to the words of the Law.*[157]

Finally, *because of him*, the people of God felt the passion he felt.

Discussion starters

Please take a look at these incidents from Nehemiah's life. Then put the number for each one where you think he was on this Kingdom Pattern when the event occurred.

1. Nehemiah weeps because of Jerusalem's plight: Nehemiah 1:4
2. The Kings gives Nehemiah authority and support: Nehemiah 2:4-9
3. Sanballat ridicules Nehemiah's work: Nehemiah 4:1
4. Nehemiah answers his critics: Nehemiah 6:8
5. The wall in completed: Nehemiah 6:15-16
6. Nehemiah comforts the people as they weep: Nehemiah 8:10

What is a key principle you see in Nehemiah's trench-shaped journey?

Please share the principle on social media using: #kingdompatterns

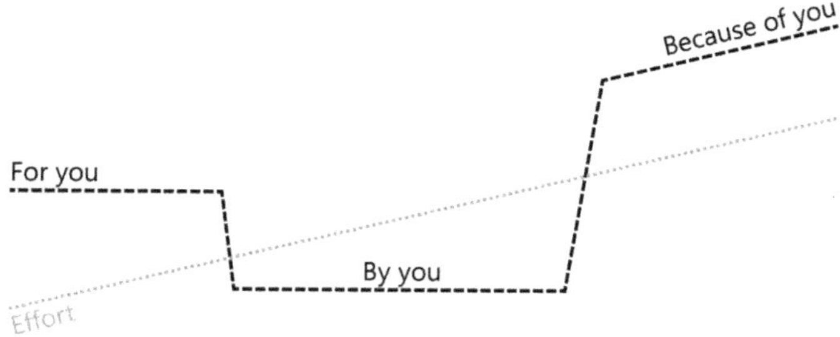

TRENCH | The Practices

Foundations

Practice #1: *Know where to find the details of His design!*

Details are provided. Details are within reach. Details are nearer than you think.

When something is built, time is taken to prepare the appropriate substructure. The taller the building, the deeper the foundation that is required. If a construction firm is erecting a house to occupy one family, then a foundation of only a few feet deep is needed. If instead, they are building an office block to facilitate one hundred people doing productive work, then a more substantial base is laid. However, if a skyscraper is intended, something that will become a landmark, something that can be seen from a long distance away, something that catches the eye, an even deeper foundation must be developed.

So the bigger the thing that God is building *through* you, the deeper the foundation He is required to build *in* you.

This can be surprising to a lot of us for one simple reason.

When apprentices join our youth leadership course, God has already done a certain amount of work in them. He has laid just enough foundation required for their voluntary help in a church youth group. However, if they are to represent Him in a school, with a larger circle

of influence and a more complicated environment, a more substantial foundation is required. The old trench is not deep enough for the new adventure. So, a new trench has to be built.

Consequently, 'the trench' will be a repeated pattern in our lives.

The foundation done in one trench earlier in our lives, may not be sufficient for the greater thing that lies ahead. However, because we already know that God has done a work in us, we think that whatever foundation has previously been built *in* us will be good enough for the next thing God builds *through* us.

But we are wrong.

So let me encourage you, when looking for God's next step, don't look up . . . Look down.

You are more likely to find the details of God's direction when you are seeking the things He wants to do *in* you rather than *through* you. Therefore, rather than looking for what He seems to be hiding from you right now, common sense says it is better to grasp what He is teaching you right now. Instead of constantly asking "What does He want to do through me in the future?" notice what He is saying He wants to do in you now. These things will be easier to spot.

You see, God rarely shows us exactly what He intends to build *through us* and yet seems very happy to tell us exactly what He needs to build *in us*! Or to put it another way:

> He gives us a *generic* design for the building, but a *specific* design for the foundation.

Joel

Practice #2: *Don't be limited by a reward!*

Rewards dilute us. Rewards distract us. Rewards divert us.

One day, when my eldest son was seven years old, I took the family to the local indoor pool. I'll never forget the moment Joel came up to me and said, "Dad, I think this is the day I can do it. I think I can go farther than I have before."

I was excited—he wanted to swim the entire length of the pool! As a parent, I knew this was going to be one of those defining bonding experiences and so I encouraged him, "We can do it, son! We can do it together!"

"But Dad," he said, "I'm nervous. I'm really, really nervous. I want to do it, but I need some encouragement. Maybe if I make it, I can get some kind of reward."

"Like what?" I asked him.

"A PlayStation," he replied.

After a short time of negotiations, and the promise of a secondhand PlayStation, we dove into the pool together. Joel started strong and I was proud. Then he began to struggle and I was concerned.

"It's hard, Dad! It's hard!"

"Come on, son, you can do it!" I replied.

"Is there anything else, Dad? Anything else I could have if I make it?"

We treaded water together with one third of a length to go. "What about a game to go with the console?"

Inspired by these rewards, Joel, my hero, pushed through the pain barrier and his fear and made it to the end of the pool. I cheered and hugged him. Grabbing his hand, I ran to his mother, excited to tell her what we had accomplished together. I gushed to Lynn of his wonderful feat, his courage, his determination to go beyond his limits, his swimming of his first full length. I will always remember her face as she looked me deep in the eyes and said:

"Paul, he's been able to do that for six months!"

She went on to explain that half a year ago he swam a length and received his official certificate. I looked down and there was my son, a big smile on his face, the promise of a PlayStation and game firmly secured, his face the epitome of what the English call . . . 'cheeky.'

Joel's primary purpose that day was *not* to see how far he could go, but to see how much he could get. Therefore he only went as far as he needed to gain a reward. In the same way, we can limit ourselves to only fulfill the calling that brings a title, finance, and praise, instead of taking a path that would be more effective for the Kingdom.

Sometimes, like Joel, we give the appearance of going further than we really can.

Cap

Practice #3: *Flip a weakness to discover a new strength!*

It brings motivation. It brings stimulation. It brings cohesion.

A former president of the USA told the story of how, as a young boy, he loved to climb. He would climb anything, trees, houses, hills—whatever was set before him. Yet there was one wall that he passed every day on his way to and from school that was so high that he was always too scared to attempt. The months went by and each time he walked passed his nemesis, he would say to himself, "One day I will climb that wall."

Yet he never did.

Now, his family was very poor and he was always taught to look after everything he was given. Rich people don't always have the same appreciation for things that poor people often do. So if he lost something, he broke something, or he forgot something, he would be disciplined, usually physically, by his father.

His school uniform was especially sacred and he was commanded to take extra care of it.

The end of term came, and as he walked to school on the last day, he passed the wall, thinking, *Today is my last chance*. Yet he kept on walking. Like many of us, he was trying to figure out how to make himself do something he had never been able to do before. Then on his final trip home past his nemesis, an idea struck him.

He threw his school cap over the wall!

Once he had done this, there was no going back. He had to retrieve it in order to save himself from a beating. It forced him to do something he had previously lacked the courage to do, and he finally did what he had never previously been able to do.

Sometimes to lead ourselves into a new phase of life, we have to throw our cap over the wall. We have to make a commitment that will force us to do what is required of us. That may look different to you than me. I have a strong sense of responsibility and a position of leadership that requires me to be a good role model. So if I promise people something, I am highly motivated to not let them down. Therefore, 'to throw my cap over the wall,' I tend to make public statements that force me to do things I don't want to do.

For instance, a couple of years ago, to bring more discipline to my devotional life, I went through a season of blogging my personal morning Bible study every day. Before I changed to a new system, I had written commentaries on six books of the Bible!

As you stand on the verge of a potential trench, let me ask you a question:

What is the wall you are facing, and what could be *your* cap?

Discussion starters

Practice #1: *Know where to find the details of His design!*
Practice #2: *Don't be limited by a reward!*
Practice #3: *Flip a weakness to discover a new strength!*

1. Which of these practices seems most relevant to you at this point in your journey?

2. What is the next practical step for you to take?

3. What questions do you still have?

4. What advice that I have not written would you give someone journeying on this pattern?

5. Please share your advice and questions on social media using: #kingdompatterns

The Progress of a Pilgrim

Fleece

There is a practice common to Christians that summarizes a lesser way to find God's direction.

It is based on the story of Gideon's fleece, and the story goes like this. God sent a messenger to Gideon and told him that he would defeat his enemies if he attacked them with God's strength. Gideon, however, needed assurance, and so he made a rather odd request:

> *Gideon said to God, "If you will save Israel by my hand as you have promised—look, I will place a wool fleece on the threshing floor. If there is dew only on the fleece and all the ground is dry, then I will know that you will save Israel by my hand, as you said."*[158]

God graciously answered him, giving Gideon the sign he asked for.

Yet that was not enough.

> *Then Gideon said to God, "Do not be angry with me. Let me make just one more request. Allow me one more test with the fleece, but this time make the fleece dry and let the ground be covered with dew." That night God did so. Only the fleece was dry; all the ground was covered with dew.*[159]

Gideon's request was not an act of *faith* but an act of *fear*.

Yet, strangely, some of us follow Gideon's example. We set out 'fleeces' for God. We look for direction in the turn of events and, without realizing it, we essentially follow omens just like the pagans did. Instead of acting on what we know God has said through His Word, we say to Him, "If this happens then I know you want me to do such and such; if it doesn't then I know you don't."

We fall foul of seeing signs in everything, and we see more significance in circumstances than we should. It can get confusing and can cause us to subconsciously stack the odds in favor of the answer we want to hear.

Yet this is not my main concern with 'fleeces.'

My biggest problem is best explained when describing a common scenario in my married life. The Foxy Lynn and I have been wed for twenty-seven years. Now, imagine that one day she walks into the living room as I am using the remote control to flick through the TV channels. She sits down and waits for me to choose a station.

There are three possible choices:

> The cooking channel where Jamie Oliver is creating a fifteen minute culinary masterpiece.
>
> The home improvement channel where a couple are choosing to *"love it"* or *"list it."*
>
> The soccer channel where England is losing a penalty shoot-out to Germany.

Now, imagine if I thought to myself, *I wonder which channel she would like to watch*? And then decided: *I know! If she sits down and crosses her legs, it must be the cookery show, but if she curls up on the sofa, it's the home improvement channel. However, if she scratches her head, then obviously she wants to watch the soccer.*

That would be ridiculous, right?

I love Lynn, I have grown to know Lynn, I know which channels she would prefer. You might think that presenting the three options demonstrates that I care about her and her wishes, but I'm not so sure she would see it that way. I know that even asking her what she would like to watch will induce 'the look.'

In her mind, *If you know me, you will understand me.*

Yet this bizarre routine is exactly what we are relying on when we put 'fleeces' before God.

I am sure that some of us have used 'fleeces' and can point to the fact that God answered our questions in the same way that he did with Gideon. That would not surprise me. God is faithful. More than that, He meets us where we are. He reaches down to our level and guides us as children. He is, after all, a very loving father. That does not mean, however, that He wants us to stay infants for the rest of our lives. So God may occasionally honor our fleeces, but what are they saying about our desire to get to know Him? And what difference is there between our Christian fleeces and a pagan's omens or a witch's crystal ball?

I think there is a better way.

A practice that makes His thoughts our thoughts, His dreams our dreams, and the passion of His heart the passion of our hearts. I believe that God does have a plan to prosper you and not to harm you, but that this plan is best recognized through the *tupos* of His Kingdom Patterns.

Can I therefore encourage you to practice asking questions? After all, vision comes from an awkward conversation with God. The drama of signs and wonders simply gets our attention but gives little revelation. Signs are used to pull us into a dialogue with the Father, whereby we ask Him a question and He replies with one. While the questions keep coming, so does the revelation. When the conversation stops, the vision stops.

This practice of 'perpetual conversation' leads to the progress of a pilgrim.

It begins with the question:

What is the most effective thing I can do for God's Kingdom?

But when that question becomes your default inquiry, you are moving further into His purpose for you. The conversations that then follow help you to remember the most important thing about your journey as a pilgrim . . .

In Joseph's slavery, Peter's betrayal, Israel's rebellion, and Nehemiah's persecution, God never left them. He continued to journey with them because He always journeys with pilgrims. You can be going the wrong way, but His presence does not disappear. Even when you are on the wrong path, you will continue to see the signs of God's activity in your life. God's provision and His blessings are not always an indication that we are going the right direction; they are simply His way of showing us He still loves us. And He does still love us, even when we mess up and choose a path that we should not.

Therefore, the purpose of the question is never: "Will God journey with me?"

It is always: "Will I journey to Him?"

NOTES

Endnotes

1. For more insight on the concept of the line, see another book in this trilogy, Kingdom Pioneering (Colleyville, TX: Harris House Publishing, 2017).
2. Revelation 1:7.
3. 1 Thessalonians 4:17.
4. Ecclesiastes 3:11.
5. According to the Jewish law, there were three feasts that all Jews should attend in Jerusalem: Passover, Pentecost, and Tabernacles. Due to distance, Joseph and Mary, like many others, could only attend one of them. So they chose the biggest and best; this meant that as they journeyed home they traveled with a large caravan of extended family and other companions. It is easy to get lost in a crowd and their son was not where they expected Him to be.
6. Luke 2:41-43.
7. Luke 2:44.
8. The Oxford English Dictionary entry for "pilgrim, n."
9. Genesis 12:1-3.
10. See the Bunting Clover Leaf map at http://paulgibbs.info/map-excerpt-latest-book.
11. Genesis 17:5.
12. Keren Hannah Pryor, A Taste of Torah (Dayton, OH: Center for Judaic-Christian Studies, 2008).
13. Romans 12:2.
14. Jeremiah 17:9.
15. G3339 Strong's Concordance.
16. Philippians 3:17 NIV 1984 ed.
17. This definition is an amalgamation of tupos and the combination of base words it is derived from.
18. Encarta Dictionary English entry for "pattern, n."
19. Nehemiah 9:8.
20. Psalm 18:35 NIV 1984 ed.
21. Psalm 18:36 NIV.
22. Psalm 18:36 NLT.
23. Psalm 18:36 KJV.
24. You can read more about this story and the peculiar instance involved in the other two books of this Kingdom Trilogy, Kingdom Pioneering and Kingdom Principles.
25. Hebrews 12:1 MSG.
26. Genesis 37:5 MSG.
27. Genesis 37:6-7.
28. Genesis 37:28 NLT.
29. Genesis 37:36.

30. Genesis 39:2 NLT.
31. Genesis 39:7-20.
32. Genesis 39:19-20 NLT.
33. Genesis 39:22-23.
34. Genesis 40.
35. Genesis 41:1-40.
36. Genesis 41:45 NLT.
37. Genesis 41:41 NLT.
38. We see this demonstrated in the story of Jacob at Bethel in Genesis 28.
39. This is taken from The Hayford Bible Handbook (Nashville, TN: Thomas Nelson, Inc., 1995).
40. Genesis 37:19.
41. Genesis 40:9-18.
42. Genesis 41:14-16.
43. Genesis 37:10.
44. Genesis 16:1-2 NLT.
45. If you have read the two previous books in this trilogy, you will realize that the school did not turn out to be what she expected.
46. I'm guessing in today's prices that is just under $5.
47. When I started to write books, I chose to include my middle name in memory of my mum and her belief in me.
48. Psalm 30:1.
49. Psalm 30:6-7 MSG.
50. This quote is often attributed to Abraham Lincoln, and appears to derive from his quote, "Nearly all men can stand adversity. But if you want to test a man's character – give him power."
51. John 12:12-13 NLT.
52. In 73AD, the Roman army lay siege to a remnant of Jewish zealots who originated from northern Galilee at the mountain fortress of Masada. Masada was an almost impregnable stronghold built by Herod to protect him from Cleopatra. With resistance to a siege in mind, it was built with deep cisterns to store thousands of gallons of drinking water and pigeon holes on its roof in order to keep the birds for meat. Yet the Roman Empire spent months building a ramp and just when they were on the verge of breaking into the Zealots camp, their intended victims seemed to have made a staggering decision. They drew lots, picking ten soldiers who knew about killing. The fathers killed the families, the ten killed the fathers, and one killed the ten and then committed the final suicide. Today, the Israeli army takes its new recruits to Masada when they pledge their allegiance to protect the nation.
53. John 18:15-16 NLT.
54. John 18:25 NLT.
55. John 18:19.
56. Matthew 14:22-33.

57. Matthew 16:13-23.
58. Matthew 17:4-8.
59. Matthew 17:20 NLT.
60. Luke 5:4.
61. To see another angle of the story connected with this one, check out the section 'Boat' in another book in this trilogy, Kingdom Principles (Colleyville, TX: Harris House Publishers, 2017).
62. To hear from my Pastor about this whole process, please watch the documentary about The Pais Movement at www.thespiritofapioneer.com.
63. A quote by Sydney Coe Howard, a famous American playwright.
64. Matthew 17:4.
65. William McBirnie, *The Search For The Twelve Apostles* (Wheaton, IL: Tyndale House Publishers, 1973).
66. Luke 3:21-22.
67. Job 1:9.
68. Oasis. "Some Might Say" *(What's the Story) Morning Glory?* Writ. Gallagher, Noel. (London, UK: Creation Records, 1995).
69. Luke 3:22.
70. Tosefta Sotah 13:2.
71. Notice that at Jesus' baptism, *Bat-Kol* was used to communicate to the onlookers, not Jesus Himself.
72. Colossians 1:24.
73. Genesis 2:18.
74. Ephesians 4:11-13 NIV 1984 ed.
75. Some of you may no longer believe these gifts are still present today. Please let me encourage you not to let that deter you from seeing the pattern. They are just an example.
76. Ephesians 4:13.
77. Ephesians 4:14.
78. Luke 3:23.
79. Matthew 11:12 NLT.
80. Matthew 4:12, 17.
81. I personally do not fully subscribe to this.
82. Hebrews 5:8 VOICE.
83. The Pharisees were a progressive party. Unlike the Sadducees, they knew that religion must move forward and not stand still. They did not set themselves up as the only interpreters of religion like the Sadducees. The Pharisees insisted on the right to interpret and explain the teachings of Judaism, so that all the common people could understand. They believed in the resurrection of the dead, be it in an immortal soul; divine punishment of sin; free will reconciliation; predestination; and the existence of angels and spirits. For this reason, we very often find Jesus as a guest in a Pharisee's dinner party, but we never see him hanging out with Sadducees.

84. Luke 13:31-35.
85. Matthew 23:2-3 NIV 1984 ed.
86. A full list of these can be found on page 169 of Brad Young's book *Meet the Rabbis* (Peabody, MA: Hendrickson Publishers, 2007).
87. Matthew 7:10-11.
88. Abot 5:18, according to page 266 *The Parables* by Brad Young. For more information on Jesus use of common parabolic themes read Brad Young's book The Parables: Jewish Tradition and Christian Interpretation (Peabody, MA: Hendrickson Publishers, 1998).
89. The late Professor Flusser, who was a professor of Early Christianity and Judaism of the Second Temple Period at the Hebrew University of Jerusalem, emphasized these connections throughout his book 'The Sage of Galilee'. He is also quoted on page 63 of Brad Young's book *Meet the Rabbis* responding to a Jewish student offended by Flusser's esteem of Jesus teachings. In that book, along with his book on *Parables,* Young also highlights Jesus' use of the sages' teaching style.
90. I unpack the connection between the Amidah and The Lord's prayer in my book *Kinfdom Principles* in the section 'Amidah.'
91. Lapide, Pinchas *The Sermon on the Mount: Utopia or Program in Action?* (Maryknoll, NY: Orbis, 1986) p. 10.
92. Mishnah Berakhot 5.1 quoted in *Meet the Rabbis* (referenced above) on page 19.
93. Luke 10:4.
94. This practice involves the concept of 'Kavanah' which I teach in my book *Talmidim*.
95. Acts 9:40.
96. Matthew 5:40 NIV 1984 ed.
97. This was unpacked in the CNN report 'Fareed's Take: I was the target of internet trolling' on January 17th 2016.
98. Brian D. McLaren, *The Secret Message of Jesus* (Nashville, TN: Thomas Nelson Inc., 2006).
99. 1 Corinthians 5:11.
100. Galatians 2:11-12.
101. This was a statement I once heard made by Paul Scanlon, a church minister from Bradford in the UK.
102. Luke 5:7.
103. Roy Lloyd, a Lutheran minister, once interviewed Mother Teresa. He asked her, "What's the biggest problem in the world today?"
104. Matthew 5:46 NIV.
105. Matthew 5:46 MSG.
106. Matthew 5:47 NLT.
107. Proverbs 15:24.
108. 1 Chronicles 4:10.
109. 1 Kings 3:5, 9.
110. Mark 5:24-29.
111. See study notes in The Archeological Study Bible (Grand Rapids, MI: Zondervan, 1984).

112. Mark 5:34.
113. Malachi 4:2.
114. Matthew 23:5.
115. Exodus 1:11-13.
116. If you are unfamiliar with the story, you can find it in Exodus 1 and 2.
117. Exodus 2:11-14.
118. Exodus 3:1-3 NLT.
119. Exodus 3:5-10, abbreviated.
120. Exodus 3:11.
121. Exodus 3:13.
122. Exodus 4:10 NIV 1984 ed.
123. Exodus 4:13 NIV 1984 ed.
124. Exodus 4:18.
125. Numbers 13:27-28.
126. Numbers 14:34.
127. In fact, scholars say that while wandering, they would return many times to Kadesh, an area that acted as a base camp for their escapades. According to Easton's Bible Dictionary, one theory is that during these thirty-eight years they remained in and about Kadesh. There are eighteen Biblical references to the events that happened at Kadesh during this time. You can find a list of them in Wikipedia's Kadesh entry.
128. Proverbs 1:32.
129. Exodus 9:11-12.
130. Other examples are when He incited David to sin by numbering the army in 1 Sam 16:14. The hardening of heart of Sihon, the King of Heshbon, in Deut. 2:30 and The Gibeon Hivites in Joshua 11:19-20.
131. Exodus 7:3.
132. Exodus 1:8-10.
133. Exodus 12:38 NKJV.
134. Exodus 8:15 - also see Exodus 7:22, 8:19 and 9:7.
135. Exodus 7:3 NLT.
136. Marcus Buckingham and Donald O. Clifton, *Now, Discover Your Strengths* (New York, NY: Gallup Press, 2001) p. 145.
137. Numbers 20:11-12.
138. Numbers 13:27, 30.
139. As quoted by John Maxwell in his book *Developing the Leaders Around You* (Nashville, TN: Thomas Nelson, Inc., 1995) p. 19 with context added.
140. Nehemiah 1:2-4.
141. Anonymous.

142. Nehemiah 2:1. Nehemiah chose the month of Nisan to prompt King Artaxerxes to ask him what was wrong. I find that interesting because the original word for this month, 'Abib' means 'Green Ear'. Abib corresponds to April and was named as such because of the condition of the barley at that time. Nehemiah approached the King hoping he would have a green ear. An ear to hear and to respond with the word 'go'.
143. Nehemiah 2:1-2.
144. Nehemiah 2:2-5, 8.
145. Nehemiah 2:9.
146. Nehemiah 4:1-3.
147. You can read the lies told about Nehemiah in chapter 6 of the Book of Nehemiah.
148. Nehemiah 6:8.
149. Luke 9:62 RSV.
150. Nehemiah 5:9.
151. *Antiquities*, 11.5.8.
152. Nehemiah 11:1-2.
153. b. Katub. 110b.
154. *Antiquities*, 11.5.8.
155. Nehemiah 6:15-16.
156. Nehemiah 8:1-3, 9:2, 33.
157. Nehemiah 8:9.
158. Judges 6:36-37.
159. Judges 6:39-40.

About the Pais Movement

Our Aim

Pais exists to spark a global movement, where the primary concern of God's people is His Kingdom, and where they are equipped to advance it in their world. We do this through distinctive approaches to mission, discipleship, and study in the areas of youth & schools, churches, and business.

Our Passion

Pais is the New Testament Greek word for 'child' or 'child servant to the king.' Our motto is "missionaries making missionaries." We are passionate about the people of our world and are desperate to see them in the relationship with God that He intended us to have. We come alongside schools, churches, and businesses in their endeavor to empower people to grow in their understanding and experience of God.

Our Vision

Mission lies at the heart of Pais. We seek to help both the apprentices and those they touch develop missionary hearts, missionary skills, and missionary lives. As each missionary makes a missionary, we see our world change.

www.paismovement.com
www.facebook.com/paismovement
www.twitter.com/paismovement

About the Author

Paul Gibbs is the founder and global director of Pais. He and his wife Lynn have two sons, Joel and Levi. Originally from Manchester, England, the Gibbs family moved to the USA in 2005 to globally expand Paul's vision of "missionaries making missionaries."

Paul began pioneering openings into Manchester schools as an associate minister in 1987. In September 1992, he founded the Pais Project, initially a one team gap year project in north Manchester, which has exploded globally, training and placing thousands of missionaries and reaching millions throughout Europe, North and South America, Asia, Africa, and Australia. Since then, Paul has developed two other branches of Pais: one that equips churches in missional strategies and one that provides businesses with cause marketing strategies and cultural development. Under Paul's leadership, the Pais Movement continues to grow, launching initiatives and resources to further God's Kingdom.

Paul gained national recognition in the UK for mentoring and training leaders. He has written three books and speaks throughout the world on topics which include pioneering, leadership development, the Kingdom of God, and ancient practices for post-modern times.

Paul enjoys swimming, surfing, skiing, sailing, and snowboarding, and he is an avid Manchester United fan!

www.paulgibbs.info
www.facebook.com/paulcgibbs
www.twitter.com/paulcgibbs

To learn more about Paul's ministry, watch the documentary.

'THE SPIRIT of a PIONEER'

a film about the four stages of vision

'Inspirational & Informative!'
Based on the book "The Line and the Dot" by Paul Clayton Gibbs

TheSpiritofaPioneerFilm.com
Free to view on **vimeo**

MAKAKOH
IMAGES

Other Books by Paul Clayton Gibbs

The Ancient Trilogy

Haverim: How to Study Anything with Anyone
This unique book teaches you how to explore Scripture with those of no faith, little faith, or even another faith. Providing step-by-step guidance, Paul Gibbs equips you to launch your own Bible study using Haverim Devotions.™

Talmidim: How to Disciple Anyone in Anything
Helping us fundamentally rethink our current methods of discipleship, Paul Gibbs gives a fresh understanding of the Great Commission. By researching and applying Jesus's method of discipleship, Gibbs provides a simple template anyone can use.

Shalom: How to Reach Anyone Anywhere
Offering a fresh approach to missions, this book will help you learn how to spread the gospel naturally and effectively.

The Kingdom Trilogy

Kingdom Pioneering: Fulfill God's Calling
Presenting four stages that everyone must pass through to accomplish their God-given dreams, Paul Gibbs helps you navigate the challenges of each phase in order to fulfill God's calling.

Kingdom Principles: Develop Godly Character
Unpacking six Kingdom Principles that will transform your relationships with God and others, Paul Gibbs teaches you how to think, not what to think, in order to develop a Godly character.

Kingdom Patterns: Discover God's Direction
Offering five diagrams that show the ways in which God guides us, Paul Gibbs teaches you how to find the next step in your pursuit of God's will.

Available through harrishousepublishing.com and amazon.com.

/paulcgibbs

www.paismovement.com

CPSIA information can be obtained
at www.ICGtesting.com
Printed in the USA
FSHW021451150121
77646FS

9 781946 369284